IS A FOREIGN COUNTRY

An Anthology of Recent Romanian Poetry

Edited by Paul Doru Mugur
and Claudiu Komartin

IS A FOREIGN COUNTRY

An Anthology of Recent Romanian Poetry

Translations by: Andreea Iulia Scridon, Marina Sofia, Alina
Ştefănescu, Iarina Albu, Claudia Serea, Anca Roncea, Clara
Burghelea, Cătălina Stanislav, Alex Văsieş, Andrew
Davidson-Novosivschei and Paul Doru Mugur

The Center for Romanian Studies

Las Vegas ◊ London ◊ Palm Beach

Published in the United States of America by
Histria Books
7181 N. Hualapai Way, Ste. 130-86
Las Vegas, NV 89166 USA
HistriaBooks.com

The Center for Romanian Studies is an independent academic and cultural institute with the mission to promote knowledge of the history, literature, and culture of Romania in the world. The publishing program of the Center is affiliated with Histria Books. Contributions from scholars from around the world are welcome. To support the work of the Center for Romanian Studies, contact us at info@centerforromanianstudies.com

First Edition

Library of Congress Control Number: 2025933044

ISBN 978-1-59211-604-1 (softbound)
ISBN 978-1-59211-642-3 (eBook)

Contents

Our special thanks to Marina Sofia and Mona Momescu for their suggestions and help with editing.

If time could dream,
it would dream of itself as a poem

Paul Doru Mugur

In a world increasingly shaped by artificial intelligence, poetry is an essential form of expression that helps us preserve and nurture our humanity. The act of crafting a poem requires reflection, vulnerability, and an engagement with ambiguity—qualities that stand in stark contrast to the precision and rapid output of AI. These qualities invite us to slow down, to feel deeply, and to explore the layers of meaning of our experiences. In this way, poetry becomes not just a form of artistic expression but a practice of mindfulness and resistance against the dehumanizing effects of an overly mechanized society.

Poetry, with its intimate connection to our feelings, imagination, and the ineffable, provides a refuge for the uniquely human elements of our existence. In the Brand New World defined by Generative Pre-trained Transformer softwares and home robots, poetry stands as a beacon of our humanity, reminding us to cherish the emotional depth, the warmth of the human soul and the shared stories that define us. Without poems that touch us deeply, bringing torrents of joy and oceans of melancholy to our hearts, we risk losing the very essence of who we are.

Like love, poetry is the shortest distance between two sensibilities. It harnesses the power of metaphor, imagery, rhythm, and sound to convey emotions, ideas, and narratives in a powerful and evocative manner. Poetry emerges from lived realities, personal struggles and tragedies, and the profound need to make sense of our existence. In embracing poetry, we celebrate the mysterious, the uncertain, and we reaffirm what it means to be a human being.

Over the last two decades, Romanian poetry evolved significantly, fusing a sort of emerging "global poetics "with its strong local neo-realistic cosmopolitan sensitivity. This was the result of the free cultural exchange between Romania and Western Europe, and with the world in general, facilitated by the new technologies and the social media. The interplay between local and global influences adds depth to the poetic voices making contemporary Romanian poetry a significant contribution to the world literature.

Today, Romanian poetry is a vibrant landscape of voices and themes, reflecting the rich cultural heritage and complex social realities of our time. Romanian poets bear witness to a poetics rooted in Romanian culture but with branches spreading all across Europe and the Americas. They draw their inspiration from a wide range of sources, incorporating in their texts, elements of modernism, postmodernism, and various avant-garde movements.

The poems included here, translated specially for the anthology, are written by fifty highly accomplished young Romanian poets. The *Pain is a Foreign Country* anthology explores a wide range of sensitivities and survival strategies in our post-ironic, trans-meta-human era, where experiencing and expressing emotions has become a rare privilege. This is an extraordinary collection that we hope will appeal to all poetry lovers.

Teodora Coman

between the private truth and a universe in continuous expansion
an "I" exists, a knot of influences come from all over
obedient (t)errors of interpretation, attracted by safer and safer

black holes

that promise a pornographic ending

invisible to the small naked eye

despite the density of matter, contradicted by the void in the name.

NASA says that the Sun is not big enough to turn

into a black hole,

so it can't collapse on itself, the way we can.

praise to those who respect each other

both in harmony, and in extinction.

Translated by Andreea Iulia Scridon

the world as will and representation

whoever has well-formed reflexes
can hold a gala
even in captivity.
training keeps you in good shape,
it brings you closer to nature
where there is no such thing as obesity
from such a fight for
survival

Translated by Andreea Iulia Scridon

blinded in plain sight

the man is what he hides, without a touch of metaphor, without the iceberg
of comparison,
the body offers enough proof of restricted access:
if you want better angles or more accuracy in
self-perception, you turn to your cell phone and all you need is
someone else to film you, to contribute to your complete image.
if you see yourself from behind, the strategy and tools are even more complicated:
two mirrors instead of one, as in a barbershop, phones with two
cameras incorporated and an option for a panoramic setting.
skin wears us even when we call it naked: true
vulnerability is weighed in the weight of lost blood, in the deviation
from the rule of the closed circuit.
untouched by the lesson on truth and its path towards light,
the organs function as they know best, in sealed off
darkness. only doctors come to know them through touching, cutting,
scarring, repairing or removing them completely.
health, the necessary quarantine for a body upon which it is not
recommended to intervene at all, and the illness, a body upon which
someone should intervene with every possible means.
even if we look at radiographies, we don't know how to read them, we are missing
the deciphering key of the specialist. *blinded in plain sight*,
captives between image and imagistics.
we like the heart only as metaphor, an emoticon or a gift even in
its most hideous kitsch version bought at a flea market, so long as we
don't see it live:
as an extracted organ, it too offers the visual shock of biological
nudity, good thing we have enough tradition to cushion it:
Asian films with scenes of maximum violence, representation of
humanity's great crimes — Cain and Abel, the head of John the
Baptist, the head of Goliath, Marat, the massacre of the innocents,
Saint Sebastian, Christ in agony, infernos as far as the eye can see,
vivisections and dissections,
documentaries about genocides, colored restorations of people and kamikaze

airplanes, live terrorism on Facebook,
we even have the trapping-machine which scatters brains from a hundred meters
away from the site of the explosion
so cinematic and unaesthetic
and we've come to film tragedies and take selfies with them.
even so, the essence has remained an error, history repeats itself
and clairvoyance isn't for everyone.
we are all beneath our time on an abstract level
but time is that which levels any flaw in the landscape
from one week to another.
the dog run over on the road still warm when I passed by it
had sandy brown fur and a partially pulverized head
which you could still trip over.
now, a few days after, when some ordinary business
brought me to this place
I found nothing but a stain. it didn't feel any different from the asphalt
under my footsteps
so there was no need to avoid it.
it had lost its smell, shape and volume
which only an eyewitness could retrace
though some say it's better for the psyche to see the same painting
with different eyes, not different paintings with the same eyes, as in my
case.
It is the beginning of July and we haven't had a normal
summer so far
but rather a succession of rain and sun
that more than anything jolted matter.
an irritating time especially for those with chronic diseases, but see
what wonders it works for death,
without a quarantine regime,
until wiping it out entirely.

Translated by Andreea Iulia Scridon

comfort zone

a click away you'll find tourist offers for exotic resorts –
turquoise waters, lounges and other bait for laziness;
until the computer leads to a staircase with stairs of polished wood, which
you're always in danger of slipping on
but this is an excuse like any other, as man is the only
animal that can make use of its own powerlessness by doing
practically, nothing
so I prefer to remain near the window, where the view is
free:
no interposed buildings, no weirder neighbor's life.
My dusting of voyeurism melts in the solar contemplation of
squat rooftops, the national highway, of gardens on a second
plane, the Teaching Staff Resource Center, of the distant blocks
from the neighborhood in which I go to work each day
and, in the distance, the hills, gentle barricades of the ground ahead
of the sky which is almost Flemish
through its richness of shades
partially overshadowed by a giant cloud,
in transit above the minute rhythms of life,
much as our moral imponderability.
they announced a rain-shower for later
i hope it's a passing summer phenomenon
which won't have the strength to become a news story.
you won't find out much from me – not the hidden diseases, nor
the temptations of the workplace, nor the wrongdoings towards which I close my
    eyes or other details pertaining to anamnesis
what point would all of this have for those who prefer the end of a day,
when everything can be erased with a sponge
by counting backwards and falling unconscious
the only state from which you can wake up completely fixed
by hands deft in anatomy, by minimally invasive dreams or
any other technological method, possibly through complete anesthesia.

praise be to the sleep which disconnects you.
upon awaking you could deliver to me any story about miracles, I'd
believe it word for word, so long as I wasn't a witness. I don't
like to be the subject of a story, only of experiments forced to pass
from mice to people in order to be considered legitimate.
I support scientific progress with all my might. I await for the list
of those hankering after extreme experiences in what concerns medication not
yet on the market. I await the legalization of euthanasia.
until then, counting backwards continues every night,
passes from zero, I consider the negative numbers one by one
until the audience no longer exists

Translated by Andreea Iulia Scridon

Dan Dediu

In my narrow field of energy and rest

All the money's been spent, let the third world war come.
All the ideals have been lost from memory, the hopes
of a quiet
future,
the love is gone —
let in the troubling decline now with its sounds
of infernal, shamanic machineries
in which I might perhaps find my freedom.

I dreamt of the third world war.
On the sky, tribes of aircrafts and astral trenches,
on the Earth, giant wooden machetes
dragged in the junkie tents of people
wearing military costumes.
I dreamt that we were being chased by a band of gypsies
in a ghetto block building -
I was passing from one apartment to another
through false, thin walls,
the interrupted lines of our imagination.
Outside you could see bombs and gunshot flutters;
bodies crushed beneath the borders' rubble,
but my nightmare was only there in the building —
to run off quickly with you hand in hand, to make sure
that you would always be safe.

Let the third world war come,
in my small field of energy and rest,
with The Madman, The Magician, The Lovers, The Tower,
The Power, the Empress.

Translated by Andreea Iulia Scridon

For most people

For most people,
poetry is romanticism or noisy desperation,
low-art, Cotard Syndrome, agony or the taming of the cunt.
The first perfume, in fact, with which she tempts you
in a Parisian bistro
smelling of fresh croissants and digital serotonin,
only to blow the scopolamine back in your face and drag
you into a filthy bathroom,
infinitely listening to the melodies of shit.
For Mick Jagger, poetry is the sonorous revenge of stone
towards an extinct species of mammoths that fucked up his face
on their way to Liverpool.
For most —
poetry is the convey of Libyan women from Gaddafi's army,
their backs turned against reality,
on a beach in the Maldives, their amphorae turned
towards the Sun —
a pacemaker of sorts.
For most, poetry is a family of tormented bats
against the velvet curtain,
a sort of fragile reconciliation with the end.

and other tarot cards that I threw out of myself
onto the cherry wood table,
that was what I was thinking.

I don't remember almost anything of what had been before —
curling up, the bicycles of naive thoughts as if in a *Tour de France*
pedaling ceaselessly to inadequacy, gloomy suffering
which after a long time
I accepted as suffering,
dances and dances on streets bursting with people,
the personality of penthouses with neon lights

blinking in a hallucinatory way, before sleep,
projected on the bedroom walls
so that I might better learn the movements of others,
empty beaches, large frames, only bonfires left
and lanterns reaching towards the sky,
or a mountaintop
where I recorded out loud, in the cold air, closer
to some absurd god
the strangest thoughts
and never cheated

Translated by Andreea Iulia Scridon

august

our naked bodies
trying
to communicate —
in love we are like two chaotic machines
with their motors
smoldering with heat
animals separated from the group
spaces as small as possible
cult movies, underground music scene
self-defense mechanisms
you, such a fragile animal
at the end of the bed
yearning for caresses, security
groupings of whispered
haikus
me, such an agitated animal that wouldn't know the difference
in a moment of blindness
if it is wrong to kill you in order to protect you?
if it's wrong to harm you from too much love?
or hatred
to rake with my claws
through and through you
following laws that apply
only and only to you

      ***

I dreamed of you
lying down on the benches of an empty car
while the train
rambled slowly towards Vatra Dornei

Translated by Andreea Iulia Scridon

Imbalances

I watched the balcony. A naked chick, tall, with kinky hair to her shoulders, was
      pouring exotic tea from a samovar. This little town seems to feed off her energy
      and suddenly obtains the aura of an agitated metropolis. A Babylon
of voices,
supermarkets, sanctuaries with her turquoise eyes.
Sky-scrapers, engines, aerodynamic machineries.

In the room various events
split up — events I have previously
dreamed of —
and this should awake within me all sorts of demons.
But I won't look for any logic. An unprecedented gadget
on which I could
press Play out of curiosity
a chaotic archive would unwind on a small screen.

In a corner in the semi-darkness: a guy who resembles Geoffrey Rush
fucks an Asian girl hardcore. Doggy style. Standing. He slaps
her ass. He bites her shoulder brutally.

In another corner: the shadows of some punks
jostling each other
as some fall over from so much horseplay.
An island of blood is formed around
their bodies. Their mothers' prayers
did not succeed in taming transformations of matter.

and the sun burned on the sky like a flame
on the stove
in the dream your voice
acted upon me like a strange force
and built up galleries of images
(as I saw in a YouTube video called
"The physics of sound creating form")

"Now I hate what I loved before"
(or you said something similar
and this scared me
when I woke up)

                    ***

when I got home
at about 4 in the morning
the mother hamster in the cage from the hallway
was killing her child sinking her teeth
into his small stomach
eating from him and moving hurriedly —
my love for you is
as stupid as this
we are like this too
uprooted in time from everything
which is good
98.4% DNA similar to that of chimpanzees
75% of DNA similar to that of dogs
how much
would we resemble two hamsters
locked up in a cage?

If someone rang the doorbell now, for a second
I'd think about the consequences,
somebody, somewhere,
would not have registered what went on here.

If someone rang the doorbell now,
I'd like to be a guy of a certain stature,
balanced, strong,
that wouldn't sway before anyone. Like those assigned
by the army
to give families bad news, after war.
To ask him about life. To fill my room with life.

Translated by Andreea Iulia Scridon

one

I don't like anything
and if I don't like anything
then I become nothing
just as one is a palindrome
it's a superior instance within me
that contours my language and judgements
towards species
and grips everything I recognize
that I once was

Dan dreams words
the hippocampus of goddess Kali
Dan has visions on hashish
a punk he's talented
spatial travel

continuous exploration
you perceive the Doppler effect
past the self-destruction stations
destroyed by ephemerides
seduction is the cutting and tender katana
of the modern samurai
beyond the Van Allen century
the more scientific data about aliens
we have
the more films we see
that imagine through collective dreams
their existence and language
the quicker we dive into
our future consciousness

it's strange how your brain yearns for a certain
structure and musical trill of words
that you can hardly explain
    me mold energy
ash
me one

Translated by Andreea Iulia Scridon

Chocolate Jesus

Happiness comes from time to time. A camel grazing slowly
on the burning sand. With the rider's head on its hump, a jukebox
of dreams. The mouth is a speaker from which Tom Waits' Chocolate Jesus
is heard, the eyes a screen on which an interminable playlist rolls. The head has
roots of Banisteriopsis caapi, drops of blood and liquified gold roll down. From time
to time happiness comes. Like a distant relative from the States, whom you know
very little about, whom you only saw on certain illegal holidays. From others' stories,
from your projections. You're in the doorway, surprised. A tall guy, dressed in a
      brownish trench coat and an Amish hat on his head, with long and thin arms,
      blue eyes.
He touches you softly on the top of your head, his eyes closed, on theta and mille-
      nary
exoduses. You are a saxophone in a smoky bar in Louisiana, a pot of quilling flowers
      on a red brick balcony in Buenos Aires, behind a naked woman smoking, an
      abandoned garret smelling of books and herbs, a lantern in a market hall, a plane
      crashed in the jungle, a melody that travels through the air, a mute old man fish-
      ing, with a black cat on his shoulder, a white rabbit hidden in a junk car yard
      that observes and jots down in a big
notebook. There's a lightning bolt within each of us, fruits that ferment and tanta-
      lize, this story is an electrical release, truffles, balls of energy, we vomit one by one
      or
simultaneously, brutally or tenderly, under so many circumstances the rider's shadow
      on the hump.

Translated by Andreea Iulia Scridon

Andra Rotaru

"I am always going home
always to my father's house"[1]

even if today this voice is foreign, I will use it. with it I'll tell you "in those days
of gross viviparous reproduction, children were always brought up by their
parents (…) eventually their minds would see things as their bodies did"[2]

the animals stood there but ignored me, watching with the indifference
of beasts my gravity defying accomplishments.

    ***

[Aurora sees the old woman's knitting needles tapping a 2/4 measure. it
gradually turns into a charming waltz in 3/4. break. a cry in pain. Aurora
is bleeding. eight 4/4 measures, very wide. Aurora starts to dance and
gets dizzy. people are amazed. Aurora twirls and wriggles as if bit by a tarantula, then
suddenly collapses.]

[and nothing could have come out of their cry. a coral reef formed
around her neck, jewels, so precious any other necklace would be
imitating its art. when she opened her mouth her teeth were blunt,
like a sea mammal's. only swans carry such defense camouflage.]

[swans—broccoli. in and out of water. neck under, they are like a silky
bouquet. broccoli. who would touch a submerged swan.]

[she pulls the leash; the animal gets out. wags its tail at her feet, moves
around the fallen skin. devilish skin, a sea devil. she takes it in her arms.

---

[1]Novalis
[2]Novalis

her body smell wakes the animal. the beast begins to wash her, unnervingly.
she lays it down and heads to the horse. the horse's huge head,
eyelids half-closed. the smell is there. millimeter by millimeter, an eyelid
opens. the horse chews the skin, then desires to be lifted. she positions
herself under the animal and lifts it. they prance synchronously, then let
their skins be weighed down.]

[let's turn our attention from legs to arms. (…) the art of gestures is
crammed in between margins too narrow, for great effects. (…) what is
lost at the level of legs will be found at the level of arms. (…) the body
is no longer a way for the soul to escape; on the contrary, it gathers
around it.]

   ***

"I wish I could fly, to see things hidden underground with my own eyes![3]"

what helps you fly in air: *a mixture of gases that form the lower layers
of atmosphere, indispensable to aerobe organisms.* underground, memory
contains every gesture.

for now, we limit ourselves to events in earth:
"We bind sheaves on fields,
with sweet wine in a jug
Tra la la la la la la la la la la la la" (*Romanian Rapsody no. 1*)[4]

   ***

we kept forgetting. I decided not to forget a certain time in my life. it's
strongly connected to sleep, air whistles, and its extensions.

at first I won't remember recent events, then, those I learned of with great
difficulty. I was told you read time on a clock by looking in the direction
you stir *mămăligă*. as a child I preferred digital clocks that played music,
usually *Love Story*.

---

[3] George Enescu
[4] lyrics by Georgeta Moraru, music after George Enescu

A berceuse is "a musical composition usually in 6/8 time that resembles
a lullaby."[5]

I associate sounds with smells. when she walks, her skins bash against
each other. I look behind her and the scent of stale life is strong.

(synesthesia—a principle according to which different sensations (color,
musical, olfactory etc.) correspond to each other in affects
       — the illness of those who feel sounds have color or smells or
that colors make noise.

will not call the doctor. stopped bathing, has not brushed teeth in over 6 months.

                    ***

space: the extremes of the body. when she moved here, there were
neglected fields all around.

told me how beautiful a woman's body seemed in the chapel, sat on the
wake table. the white carnation of her skin emanates lavender. and the
powder, cotton balls in her nostrils.

when the heart stops, through gravity, blood descends to the lower body,
livor mortis. unoxygenated cells die one by one. in about a year, the body
will be nothing but bones.

we extend the body's presence for a while. formaldehyde is inserted
through a pump, straight into the circulatory system. the stomach is completely
       emptied of its content. after death, hair and nails stop growing.

I've been carrying my fear with me since I was a child—all of the ways
I could feel sick, sores in my mouth, restrictions then requirements to be
excessive. I chewed on my lunch meat until I filled up my cheeks. I'd run

_____

[5] Merriam-Webster Online Dictionary, 2010

to the bathroom to remove the round bits in my mouth. daily, I threw out
something of my connection to her. the air let out hissed.

***

nourishment: often I'd find *mămăligă* in the tea mugs. the only familiar
thing was mold, as beautiful as the water plant I once looked after. it grew
new foam every day, let out a sweet smell. it was a lucky plant, so I took
care of it. soon the whole house started smelling of urine.

today the *mămăligă* in the tea mugs is a sign of good luck.
she serves it to us too.

if I drew the genealogical tree, I'd doodle it as a knot on a rope. a sketch
of my past dependencies drawn through a meat grinder; our fleshes mix,
cannot be without each other. when I want to run all the meat I spit out
as a child retriggers the smell of vomit, it holds me still.

***

the greatest fear is self-prophecy. to recognize nothing years later.
the dying are still waiting.
forms made of forms.
I met a dead man rising with his hand up
still.

ghosts from a young age disintegrate slowly.
my head held in palms. feet tied up.
they put me on the table, covered me. they forced me to close my eyes.

***

Stage four: death

there was a time when I'd lay a handkerchief on his body,
it was a breathless moment. his breath was non-existent,
so was the wonder of a morning when shrubs poured themselves over us.

in the background, we heard: this is the big night.

edges bent inside, humans and other creatures now perish right out of
his hand, nights on shores, ice in shipwrecks, the call of the disappeared,
traces of bodies in trenches, sleepwalking horses in a forced march, blond
children, sons, blood from sacrificed animals.

"Present present *presentness*
High mahogany bed roods &
rails do ring loop ties back
A sets down and C takes up
conformity to that uniformity
Ownership and ownership it
is a maxim of logic the Double
of the object is that I desire it."[6]

Translated by Anca Roncea

---

[6] Susan Howe, *The Midnight*.

Mihók Tamás

[herk]

he looks at me
and goes tyop he looks

again tyop and
again tyop tyop

he will swallow us all
like divine granules

(we will be swallowed like
 divine granules)

his tongue will wrap
around poles

and a small fisherman within him
will turn the rod

and all of us eucalyptus farmers
will tumble

into the fissures of saliva in a rime
of bacteria just like that

tyop tyop

Translated by Andreea Iulia Scridon

[it's so hard for me]

i dreamt the sockets of my eyes
the ashtrays of a bougie club
ash the waitresses smolder me
changing them from quarter to quarter

people danced slowly i tried with all my might
to budge my clamped fingers and
like an idiot i budged out of my dream here i am
now awake scouring for pills

it must be between 3 and 4 a.m. your r.e.m
drives me crazy & it's so hard for me
to give up those few thoughts which
begin with never

pi day has passed st. patrick's day
has passed my eyes burn spasmodically
as if i'd been called to wake up
the entire springtime of the northern hemisphere

i roll my blood up and wait
i am a werewolf with bags under my eyes
like the sapwood of a fir tree suppurating
wakefulness in its own resin

Translated by Andreea Iulia Scridon

[balance]

your nervous system
like a factory studded with japanese
gestures cut in half furnaces
cut in half set to boil
feeding millions of hikikomori
putting on noodles with pieces of tofu
your centripetal gaze counting currency
and a pink hello kitty patent
nibbles a piece from our brain each day
slowly slowly absence dissipates
the grasshopper dragging after the ark
you've only got your lighter and time
we gather round the smoking area and puff
our guts rattle through microchips
a cascade of condensed milk
we watch the sky from a dead angle

Translated by Andreea Iulia Scridon

shazam. signs of life

for you natalia i am a cooperative robot
ready to butter up your soul step by step in
a zero-adherence-zero risk mechanism

i glide easily through your kitchen on tiny tracks
soft from morning to evening my tics
you have pulverized in time you

you sit in bed with your soles pasted to the ceiling and
frame memories in little circles of smoke
it's inhuman the way you forget to cry

my platinum gloves are not handkerchiefs
natalia i'm here to plug up glances
the illusion that the migraines will eventually stop

for you natalia i'm a robot possessed
by the beast of information and without dna i generate
verses about you but i don't know you

if we ever met it was a coincidence
if you ever looked into my eyes it was a farce
the lights of heaven are very small nothing but smoke and mirrors

Translated by Andreea Iulia Scridon

happiness on her way

blessed are those who lose the thread
of the costume department
and turn the wifi off
for they shall swallow
the last kernel of popcorn
watching you [you're
a bee-eater when you make love
a satin ribbon
on the nudity of the living
see the moments of imperfection
played perfectly in spontaneous direction
of the distances [the last kernel
is the saltiest in it
our embryonic states levitate
futures in contretemps repassé
with the stick shift pulled
as you covered my tactile receptors
with tilework[no shave
november vs. no sex december
as we again settle into
sterile teahouse positions
a palm on a napkin the other
plucking at the mug's handle
what splendid creatures
padded with inertia we became
nonverbal language of
our tongues this shall open
new veiled hermeneutics
how many will crash among the lines
and how many will come back [happiness
is on her way] but where do
the voices come from

Translated by Andreea Iulia Scridon

X

When I meet people I have to be careful
not to adopt their laughter, gestures, and disposition.
I can barely control myself. I fear that one day
I will respond to the name of Peter.

Translated by Andreea Iulia Scridon

Mugur Grosu

forget-you-not flower

we are a single soul,
I tell you,
and two bodies —
this is where things got a little complicated

otherwise it becomes more and more natural to relate
to ourselves more and more
as if in a profoundly democratic, complete autonomy,
among the creatures found on both sides of the mirror

I used to email to myself
reminders to my tomorrow self
messages trapped in the glass,
beginnings of poems

I tell you
the next revolution in communication
will take place when we can call ourselves
without hitting a busy line,
when we'll respond to ourselves live
and thus create a real space for dialogue
between our past and our future

I wrote myself so often
I send texts to myself as if I were my lover
I winked at myself:
I wrote period-and-comma and closed parenthesis
so that a need for the organization

of all these voices became apparent
and put them into drawers
on one I wrote: important!
on another: don't forget!
on another: documents
the problem is that whenever I look for something
I never know in which drawer to find it,
and then I have to check them one by one,
what's important? what's urgent? what cannot be
forgotten, or postponed?
I never knew how to answer,
it all comes from the same soul,
only the bodies are different

come on, take a sip
of whiskey, or wine,
and let me close the poem
with that

Translated by Andreea Iulia Scridon

sex

she told me
that she could guess how they make love
by the way they put a cigarette out:
some do it insistently,
press it hard,
until they bend the filter, others
barely touch the ashtray, and it
just keeps on smoking until it lights up
the other butts and you have to
pour whatever you've got around over it
to put the fire out, others
just forget it there really
and light another, others
lick their thumb and index finger moist
and use them to snuff out the incandescent ember, I
told her that I quit smoking so
not a chance

Translated by Andreea Iulia Scridon

slo-mo

It's been snowing all morning, obliquely, in rays
nothing touches the earth, nothing stacks up
it's only snowing to give the wind a shape,
behold, this would be your body

I slurped a coffee behind the window
when two doves popped up flying against
the current
in the strait between my tower and the tower in front of it
the wind blows hard, so they advanced very
slowly
flying slower and slower, wing to wing
and put the entire universe on a pause for a few moments

and the flakes on the window reminded me of the white static
on a TV screen
and a video camera displayed like an antique knickknack
which I bought for next to nothing
I took it home and discovered that it had a button
that allowed you to film in slow motion, step by step,
anything
I cut the TV sound off, zapped through channels and recorded
random little fragments, from films or shows,
then I played them
and everything was poetry

Translated by Andreea Iulia Scridon

when you love

when you love it's like a gory
computer game
when all of a sudden
you see a heart appear
next to the score
and realize you gained
another life

Translated by Andreea Iulia Scridon

Paradise

on social media a cute trend was causing a ruckus,
you sent pictures of yourself
and Artificial Intelligence made you an ideal portrait
like you'd never seen,
you'd swear it was you, but irresistibly beautiful,
refined, you couldn't say what was changed,
and all you had to do was allow the AI access
to your data, to check "accept" on the terms and conditions
and that's it,
you couldn't resist,
we were all the most beautiful,
absolutely adorable,
we received and gave stupid amounts of loves,

the only problem was when we wrote,
but AI could solve that, too,
just check another box on terms and conditions,
and it rewrote your messages in real time,
and you'd swear it was you, but on your best days,
if you could ever achieve such an ideal,
sharp, intelligent, the best!
we were all so irresistible we were embarrassed
to meet in the flesh,
but AI got us out of that one, too, another check
and you had a 3D avatar, in intelligent flesh,
they'd handle all our social functions,
we'd hear about ourselves on various channels
that we're actors, authors, brilliant speakers,
and finally, the world was paradise –
we all checked the box on terms and conditions with a smile,
one by one, discree
we stepped off stage.

Translated by Andrew Davidson-Novosivschei

look

first you have to learn,
then you have to forget so you can move on,
then you get used to forgetting,
you summon it like a courier
with cash on delivery payment,
a sanitation service,
then forgetting starts coming
uninvited,
stays overnight,
then brings its toothbrush,
then a change of underwear,
slippers,
until it moves completely into you,
silently,
until you forget everything,
you will think you were the guest
and then you will get out of yourself

Translated by Paul Doru Mugur

Dan Coman

I am not who I am not

the forty-year-old man smelling of coffee
the former goal-getter of the Rebra soccer team
the cool professor of social humanities

the diversionist (an upside-down pessoa)

the little boy on the carpet
fat and well-bred
gathering flowers from the edge of the cliff

the porno poet

the lead singer from The Toader,
Nina Coman & DDD

Translated by Andreea Iulia Scridon

Diva

come closer and woo me
walk around the airport with me
show me off on TV
educate me
fuck me
forgive me
anything
just get me out of here

Apartment furnished from Ikea. Sex on a regular basis. Books. Happy
children poring over screens. Chicken drumsticks in the oven.
Thirty bags filled with handwritten paper. No bank rates, no inappropriate language.
   Forgiving, seasonal illnesses.
Home-school, home-school
(the music box covered in dust
the plush heart
the video with her masturbating)

Nice weather in this kitchen where air ends
(with its yellowed lace, smelling of mothballs and dust,
fluttering over the windowsill).
Nice weather, teacher, don't stop. At school, while students
work on their tests,
next to the stove, waiting for the water to boil for coffee or in
the living room,
at the computer, with a child on one's knee and another
climbing on the bed,
imitating Angela Gheorghiu – don't stop.
Outstanding behavior, lacking any charm, but very precise.
Equidistant in evaluation (how much longer? few years? two-three months?
tomorrow?)

Here and there someone you know, stuffed in the space of reality,
screaming in pain with his eyes closed.

A ray of light hard as a plank hits the carpeting,
the coffee mug, the aged knee.

(get me out of here as soon as possible)

Translated by Andreea Iulia Scridon

come and see:

my head is a medicine cabinet
a cool and aseptic place
the rectangle of protected plywood for safety
slip your hand in and take some fresh pills
that will immediately help you to forget

come and see:
my head is the teddy bear
soft and hypoallergenic
you can sleep with it on your lap,
you can give it to a family with a baby,
wipe the dust off it, throw it against the wall, or out the window
it will wait for you there, unmoving in the dried-justup grass

come and see:
my head is a stuffed bird
the glass fish ornament atop the TV
the porcelain princess locked up in the curio cabinet
admired by guests from a small distance
the piggy bank under the bed
waiting to be shattered in thousands of pieces

come and see:
my head is a city from the north
loneliness and silence hit harder than disease
the office crammed with idiotic and poor professors,
the deserted street, the pretzel shop,
the dry air that stuffs your eyes like flocks of wool

come and see:
my head is a superb garden of coffee trees
forgotten in a chest on the balcony, in the dead of winter
when light has no power left and the earth is already frozen

the garden of coffee trees over which snow
shakes like a blind kitten abandoned at the beginning of evening
near a fence.

Translated by Andreea Iulia Scridon

Komartin Blues

4 years after Cobalt

I was never interested in truth, beauty stays in its place
even after 40,
imagination has remained intact –
we have no serious reason to use it.
That was it, pretty much.
At the end of the day we'll stay here,
where everything that has only just begun ends suddenly,
where the air flutters emptily like a tricolor flag,
half-trapped in the closed window.
(our intelligence never rose above
the level of emptiness in our chests – anyway,
not the expression of intelligence, which we so dreamed of, and that
might have gotten us out of trouble, in time.)

we sit at the table sipping coffee, in this kitchen in Berceni
where for over 15 years we have fought useless power battles
(our above-average intelligence made us dream
and we, as all dreamers,
became intransigent and boorish,
and attacked from the most unexpected positions).

(people who read are better lovers, the studies say –
new literature never had its day)

we sit in the kitchen having coffee, as if we were lying on a blanket, on the grass
and the cigarettes sizzle around us like grasshoppers but
nature, you! like a virgin you never enthralled us
like small rooms enthralled us, or a closed door, or a turned-on laptop did –
one next to the other, unmoving, waiting
for light to spread before us and to see it
setting tinder ablaze, before we could use it.

maybe a little later, after the shower, before going out into town,
there where the sky sounds like nails popping up from slate on a roof –
maybe then.
for now just thin sheets over the fresh air,
sweating like a horse, getting in the house through the window,
on the third attempt.
otherwise, behavior learned exclusively from tutorials,
gestures to inspire parents' trust,
the audience at the Blecher poetry club, high school girls.

we'll stay here, smoking another cigarette,
listening to the little motor inside our head as it races against
the little motor in our chest,
rephrasing a few dozen times before asking: is everything
okay?
it's okay.
there's nothing left to be done.
nobody else would have followed us here.
and the discolored end of light pinned down on the wall,
under the Orthodox calendar.

Translated by Andreea Iulia Scridon

Florin Partene

Life in general

Monday
: it's five in the morning
white as a sheet
I take life to work

Tuesday
: Monday is over
a great joy
gives off green energy
I stay all day with the lights on

Wednesday
: all the problems of the ego
may as well not exist
provided the ego doesn't exist
on such days you don't get addictions
you don't get depression
nothing evanescent
just plastic filings
silently settling on the bottom of waters

Thursday
: the ego has returned
plastic doesn't matter anymore
the water is agitated
we should work harder
to calm it down

Friday
: I think I'll stop here
a week is way too long
in the correct order

Oh, my youth
I catch myself leafing through a cookbook....

Translated by Alex Văsieș

Language. Life in general

Life is a chicken
perched above the ground
on a henhouse ladder
sometimes long, always full of shit

but it's not like that

some life is clear
has emotional intelligence and a propeller
sails with an accomplished body
wrings beauty after beauty from others

but it's not like that

some life is in vain
an avenue of guts
a laundry basket full of unconscious organs
lungs for air, not for smoking
heart for blood, not for worship
and liver

but it's not like that

life, velvet for wiping glasses
the jags of critical thinking
the vibrating cilia of right thinking,
was passing fluffily

but it's not like that.

Translated by Alex Văsieș

Life when it jokes

The body has passed, life is waiting still
from now on at table with Descartes

Tobacco keeps getting better and cheaper
chemistry keeps getting easier to read
clear and distinct
: its purpose is death

I wish to God
I wish I had the muscle to move
the furniture to the fourth floor
clear and distinct
: my goal is to get to bed

I fix the toy, nobody wants it
to change the planet
to do something
clear and distinct
: I am the toy

The bed passes slowly
When it's all yours

The body has passed
Life is waiting still...

Translated by Alex Văsieș

Life in Rodna Veche

winter is coming
then through it comes christmas
after that, santa in boxes
love comes
its day passes
then love back in boxes
the bunny comes, fuck the bunny,
then the bunny back in boxes

here comes the man cub
the man cub passes
life faster than demand
and then comes of course the offer

I ask for water and I get precisely water
I ask for love and I get only love
I ask for this to stop
and I get it

I sigh because it's evening
to ask for love and get a punch,
a splendour

I'm slumped in Rodna Veche
slumped in the grass
and I write a poem

Translated by Alex Văsieş

Winter Holidays

around the winter holidays
in frozen Cluj, on Clinicilor Street
it struck me:
"everyone carrying Christmas trees in their arms
only me carrying adult diapers"

and I got emotional, I almost pushed the passers-by away
admiration and grace
I found the description
so sad, so fundamentally tragic
that I hurried to write, even sent a text,
and I got one myself: how are you?

what can I say... I was happy
the frenzy of words hadn't visited me for days
the way these mind splinters
elevate memory above cognitive processes
had not shown itself to me on Monday and Tuesday.

then suddenly I woke up
in Manasia's Cluj
mites of exhaust,
swallow and fish,
creatures unsuspected by my evolution
rushed to eat my liver
and I turned to wood
but through the wood they made their way
splinter on the Amazon, peace

then it was simple, I arrived
I adorned the waiting adult
when I spoke to him the hospital room lit up,
the machines began to play,

those who had tickets rushed in,
he's dying, I think he's passing away, but how is it possible,
I could hear the jingle bells,
a whole town singing
guts full of hope,
I wish they'd call me Claudius, Epicurus and Marcel

mine was breathing.
I never caught the end
death is coming, oh what a joy
impressed by words
I went out in Boc's Cluj
wearing a coat that didn't fit me
and an unwavering faith
I still believe that the other
had put on whatever he could find

the words remain
they bring back the dead when there's nothing left to do
he was a good man
only they can bring the end
a smell you washed away
returns with a sentence:
when I met you everything smelled like Christmas trees
then like you
and it lasted a long time.

In the winter you must write
to say something,
everyone with Christmas trees growing in their palms.
I rush to you like the whole planet does to the supermarket,
to think
"Hi, I'm Florin and I've been clean
for 10 years"
and your memory to remember seamlessly

the flower of silence in my vase,
seriesofwordsweare
splinter on the Amazon,
peace.

Translated by Alex Văsieş

Livia Ștefan

Nights in This City

How does it hurt when it hurts?
Do you feel your hair falling,
your nails growing?
When it rains, do you too turn your face to the sky?
When no one is around, do you press on your eyelids?
If someone calls you from a thousand kilometers away
can you spot the place where the cry originated?
Are you the most silent of humans?
How does it hurt you
for whom do you grieve,
the dead or the living?
What are you reaching for?
I walk through this city
at night
buy a pack of cigarettes
smoke them
know that this is how the day ends
with no regrets, anger, despair
I try to figure out why it's so busy and noisy
all this pettiness
everyone talking at once
all the bodies yearning in their sleep
all lying there like vegetables
awaiting their turn to be chopped
dropped into the pot
dreaming of yet another bad day and someone
whispering in their ear
how does it hurt you?

I walk night after night in this city
buy some cigarettes
smoke them all.

Translated by Marina Sofia

The Cage in the Animal

This is how you end up
and all the love
all love in this world
presses against you

And all the love
all love in this world
passes you by
and rattles the bars of the cage
with a wooden stick

Translated by Marina Sofia

Room 211@ #Tracesofdelight

Traces of enchantment on these streets, night time, the sudden taste of nostalgia on the grand boulevards, the way the light rushes through the city, frenetically, crossing entire neighborhoods like a river made up of telephones, cars and windows, barely discernible in its intermittent flow, bringing all known residues and appetites from which you will never recover, bad nights, hot, stinking of confusion, all the mind traps transfigured into the shapeless patterns of ice cubes – a language that dissolves and dilutes history. The nights dissolve and dilute the survivors. Summer with its speculative fiction and the strategic awkwardness of bar encounters, people arriving with drooping shoulders, hanging onto their barstools, tapping a sinuous rhythm with their fingers on the shiny counter, stroking the rims of their glasses, smoldering in their unconventional reveries, consuming themselves slowly, indecently, irrationally alone.

Translated by Marina Sofia

The Doll

Drooping by the light switch
as if she were the most beautiful woman in the world
her dress riding up her thighs
a girl sits smoking
a joint.

just give me these small pleasures
I wouldn't know what to do with a big one.

Translated by Marina Sofia

Room 409. Direct Investments in Tourism per Capita.

You're growing
far away from the opium poppy fields
far from the sea glass beaches
some days pass
calmly, precisely,
like an impeccable legal contract
but the beast is always near
so near
and on some nights it falls
onto your bedsheets
meticulous bots of insomnia
like the fishermen's nets
sinking decisively into the Danube

You're growing
in clichés and common places
far from the land-mined fields
far from the verandas soaked in heat,
languor and the smoke of Cuban cigars

You're growing
into a brute
too mature, too naïve,
too alone
the beast is always near
you learn to pluck
Colorado beetles off
the potato-shoot
and throw them one by one
into the chipped basin
to crush them afterwards on the garden path
you learn to recognize spirits
by their aromas or by their absence

You're growing alongside
your liver, your cholesterol, oblivion.
You're growing together with
your days of punching in at work
your bank loans
your neighbor's children who've grown up and left
hidden in crooked bodies
irritable and irrational minds
second-hand cars and light clothing
panic attacks and phobias
Growing offers of perfect vacations
growing pile of bills
growing number of supermarkets and parking places
and distance between people

You're growing your selection of TV programs
the number of followers on social media
the speed of alienation
and the silence
the beast is always near
softly breathing

You're growing your thirst for power and abuse
the spare tire around your waist
your credit card debt
the bone spurs in your vertebrae
you have 10, 20, 40 years to spend
in the shadows, anonymous, banal,
engaged in useless equations, small wins,
contaminated blood, paltry gestures,
pictures on the cigarette packs, toothless nightmares,
you encounter exhaustion, manipulation,
self-motivation, failure,
the sublime indifference of brilliant minds

oh wait.
You learn to lock your door,
turn down the music, read
your philosophers in chronological order,
save water and reduce your electricity consumption,
cultivate your habits,
control everything,
create a false sense of isolation,
say to your weary heart
oh wait.
10, 20, 40 years of shrugging,
certified copies, grimaces,
prescriptions for antibiotics,
pockets waiting to be filled,
you grow with champagne dreams
and a lemonade budget.
Salary growth, taxes growth,
grow your own chicken
burn it on your own barbecue grill
grow irises, tulips, couch grass on your graves
a growth in cybercrime cases
growth in drug consumption,
rapes, documentaries about poverty,
asylum requests, fake news,
the upgrades in your security systems,
terrorist attacks,
the number of migrants,
the number of conferences,
the cost of therapy,
insurance premiums, unemployment figures,
house prices,
the rat population in our sewers,
pension contributions and the walls between nations,
forgotten friends, optical prescription,
hyper-reality, lack of social communication,

discrimination,
loneliness,
diseases
and the fear of death.

Far away in the fields
of absinthe and hallucinogenics
in serotonin lakes
and peaceful valleys of love
far, far away
the little beast
is still there.

Translated by Marina Sofia

Domnica Drumea

***

i thought the tram would turn left
on chitila way i was waiting for it to toss me lightly
to the left when the road turns right
and on the right when it turns left i was almost
    sure it would turn left on chitila way
when i saw the rails flowing into one other
like a memory flowing into another memory
like the danube into the sea like mom's birthday on women's day
    then i realized, gabi,
that i would have stayed up late with you at night to get on
    together
on the tram floating elegantly down the rails with no
    fear of intersections
our stories intersected over the table in
    the old pastry shop by the name of cireşica
now transformed into a noisy cafe where
    you have to scream in order to be heard
i would have stayed with you and i wouldn't have slept still dressed without
    the energy
to even wipe my makeup off
or maybe just not caring that
    my story
intersects with the city's 2 million people
    these 2 million rails
woven into a silver network that never falls
i was waiting for tram # 20 to toss me lightly to one side
    or # 45 or any tram at any
intersection where hyacinths are attacked by greedy

bees and i don't know who
i have to give priority to you or to the flowers or to the impatient black mercedes
     or to the angry voices
on the phone i was waiting for a tram at the end of the line to
     take me left, or right or
straight ahead.

Translated by Andreea Iulia Scridon

Purity

on the day when i don't want to get up
as if from in a coffin made of ice

i will die with a dry and old heart
as all people have

i read about purity
it is the only thing that can take any form
and the only thing that can destroy any form
just like my brain
apathetically destroys
any command to the hand
prepared to caress

Translated by Andreea Iulia Scridon

Snow

my life is an endless field of snow,

in front of the window, i tell you that the snow erases everything,

all traces.

i broke the mirror which shows me whole,

i can't stand myself.

don't ask me why my left hand hits objects,

i can't stand myself.

my life is an endless field of snow.

make love as if you were locked inside an iron virgin.

laugh until you are exhausted.

replace one severed head with another

and your arms embrace me violently and place me among objects.

the sun like an incision in the winter sky.

push the limits of self-control, know the exact dose,

all you have to do is not fall asleep.

i am an endless field of dirty snow.

i delete everything.

all traces.

Translated by Andreea Iulia Scridon

***

I live at the mercy of the government

unconscious and frustrated
like poultry in the yard

dependent on physical
and mental stimulants

how long can i bear
a flashing light

the placid beauty of an industrial landscape

obsessed with self-control
and safety
i change irreversibly

someone will come and train me
they will teach me to drop food on the floor

Translated by Andreea Iulia Scridon

***

my ambition is failure

i advance through the victories of others
as through a colony of jellyfish

nothing to blind me
and destroy me

programmed to tick only the wrong answers
i turn my back
to the mercy and its followers

i set an anonymous target
in movement

increasingly cruel
more and more deviant

use my body
blow hot air over me

Translated by Andreea Iulia Scridon

Diana Geacăr

superpowers

You can live without sex, but not without touch, says
a woman with wrinkled skin in a show about

health, as I pick up the laundry from the balcony.
Since I gave birth, my husband has had a cold

several times. I haven't even had one.
The first thing I do in the morning is to

put my wedding band on my finger. Passing from perfect
baby skin to the partner's used-up skin

is difficult, says the woman. My husband smiles
at our child, then goes to his room. The rain raps

on windows with the fury of bodies desperate
to get in. I saw crocodiles standing dead-still

in the water while they were caressed
by people, monsters with repulsive skin,

powerless. My son, who I always hold in
my arms, stretches a hand out from his crib

and says Aaa. A shadow probably
caught his attention. I remain stone still in the doorway, laundry in hand,

when I realize that he's smiling at me. The first thing
that I do in the morning is to become invisible.

Translated by Andreea Iulia Scridon

Some things are so terrifying that they seem invented

A giraffe crushes a lioness under its feet, then madly
searches for its offspring. It doesn't know that the man

was filming. Frantically, it tries to feed
all the giraffe babies that cross its path.

Some lionesses watch helplessly as flesh
of their own flesh is detached from bone by the rival herd.

An antelope mother struggles and flounders, its legs
like little branches, in order to remove her child

From the trunk of a snake. She's got no chance, sadly says the man
who didn't get to film the beginning. A penguin wrestles

to lift its head from under the belly of a sea lion and
pinch its chest. Around them, a circle of penguins

stands and watches. At the end I saw signs of penetration,
says the man overwhelmed by the scenes offered to him.

It's raining outside, I rifle through the bed looking for a hippopotamus head.
Piece by piece, we too travel through the savanna.

Two flamingoes and a crocodile bathe in a lake.
A couple giraffes chuckle through the branches of a

tree. A snake coiled on a bough winks
at us. My son screams and kicks his legs.

Savanna is cut piece to piece, the animals hide among the bedsheet,
under the bed, beneath the shelter of imagination. I cover my coffee.

Translated by Andreea Iulia Scridon

From the other side of The Moon

...at the instant I disappear behind the moon, I am alone now, truly alone, and
absolutely isolated from any known life. I am it.
Michael Collins, astronaut on Apollo 11

There are three images that contain such a great secret
that I wouldn't understand it even if

Morgan Freeman explained it to me. I dreamt the first two.
I don't believe the third, not even now.

In the first, I'm sitting on a hill at night and see the Earth
on the sky so close and so beautiful that my eyes

hurt. On the second, I'm in a muddy field, I look around
and don't see anything but a weak light, greenish but a long

scream made me lift my gaze. An enormous animal, maybe
a whale, passes cleanly above me, through dark waters.

In the third I pass the day in a chapel and look at
my father. I put my hand on his chest. Death has made him resistant.

The gravediggers will pull him around like the wrong
plank, because they forgot to put his beret on.

Daddy, I say, trying to establish a relationship
with the object. Maybe I'm in a documentary

about submergence. In fact, there are four images.
A woman floats motionless in murky water and gazes

through the metal fishnet into the eyes of a crocodile.
When she emerges to the surface, she starts to cry and wakes

my baby up, who sees me, but smiles
only a few seconds later.

Translated by Andreea Iulia Scridon

One, two, three, four, five,
once I caught a fish alive

When you tell the truth, people open up
like a crocodile's jaws. Missus, miss,

a salesgirl asks me with an
encouraging gaze, but I, since I haven't decided

what I want, I stay quiet as the universe, thrilled that we
incidentally breed confusion. Actually, I don't have enough money.

Translated by Andreea Iulia Scridon

We are parents, we are pure

When the child is around, we don't speak to each other
except when we are absolutely sure

that we have removed all the dangerous pieces.
I need you, I tell my husband, who

gets up quick from the computer screen and comes to bed,
where our son awaits him, undressed. He takes him to the bath,

holding him from a distance, and, while I wash him, we touch
each other, smiling. Because every toy with dead

batteries, if left alone, will still work
enough to have its legs spread from time to time.

Translated by Andreea Iulia Scridon

Animommy

The calendar says another month has passed.
We have to take its word for it.

Humankind cannot bear very much reality,
wrote T.S.Eliot. My son sits on me

as if on an armchair. I take a sip of coffee, then I tell him,
without hesitation, what the geometric shapes that appear

one by one on the television are called. There are no
straight lines in nature. And from here, down here, we see the square

of the window, behind which a pine tree
flounces. If I turned with my face towards him,

I wouldn't see him. That's about how
I understand reality. Animommy, he says.

Translated by Andreea Iulia Scridon

Presence

Given the dimensions,
I can
stay here, or there
from this point of view
it makes no difference,
yet it makes
a difference.
From this *point of view*
the point of view
passes
or commutes
and the halving begins to collapse
COLLAPSE?
only on the blind through the thin dust
ashy sun gentle snow
a nostalgia of sorts
people who type with care
speak to each other and to me
TO ME?
Of course, to me too
but this makes no difference
or maybe it makes the smallest *difference*
the smallest implosion
in what is
but what is
is nothing
man speaks of the
PRESENT
be here now
be here now
he nods
but softly
the balloon head
doesn't know that much.

Translated by Andreea Iulia Scridon

Ligia Keşişian

The waiting room

A new night from a new year
awaited like a train in a village
and I saw the moon too
one spring in the '90 when
I set off barefoot on the road with my eyes
closed at the edge
of a ravine
the dogs started to bark at me
from the valley,
that was when I bit
a piece of the moon as if it were a giant butter cookie
I jumped between planets
light as the cold
for a while I stayed
outside of time and sleep
I ate raw potatoes on the field
and smoked cigarette buts thrown
near people's houses
childhood's games had become levitation
above the red river
I picked thistles off animals' fur
and looked for worms in the wet dirt
one day
a blind man and a spineless woman appeared
a handful of knotted snakes
show them the way
they told me they wanted to find the sun in the heart of the earth

they entered
to bathe in my embers
in which small animals
willfully perished
for a while I fed them raw fish
the snakes were tame they slept on my back
I never slept
but hopped from one planet to another
that was when I really existed
in that new night from a new year
I broke the rabbit's head and asked myself
for the first time
what it means
to d i s a p p e a r.

Translated by Andreea Iulia Scridon

Eat me

I told myself
stop thinking about everything
a reason for morality
is a resin stain that darkens

I was afraid of
the prophetic aspect of my
older poems that everything
that I would write
would happen

among 4 walls around the body
shrinking like an ice cube
and what

this superpower of equilibrium means

and how my own words
ever helped me and what
is there to explain and to who
since everything melts and drips and passes

my failure
and my flesh's
and my tongue's
failure
of clinging to solid options
and how much waiting
a heart spinning in a chest,
a dancer captured by flames,

and why is it only memory
that grows like a fattened pig
until its skin bursts.

Translated by Andreea Iulia Scridon

Winter games

I would have liked for us to have had
the perfect synchronicity of ice-skaters
their state of floating
liquid and sparking ligaments
in slow-motion

hunched over a coffee listening
to the scratching of blades
among motionless bodies and wild animals
we hear blood as it always flows from the brain
and transports the wrong information deficiencies of iron and courage

in case of an emergency smash the window with your head
if you feel a heart attack coming on, take out any old heart
from any old chest and bite it
torrential rains shall set in

someone knocks at the door
and tells me — you don't have to go so far away
tells me to be a good girl
my blood flows in every direction
like that of a Bengalese tiger ready for attack

Translated by Andreea Iulia Scridon

***

every intention creates effervescent bubbles in parallel worlds
on certain nights I grow within me almost human settlements
populated by very tall and thin inhabitants
superstitious and tender
on certain nights I lie down on the streets
and cover massive surfaces with my body

some things just can't be spoken outlaid

read the signs carefully
to resurrect or to become extinct is a matter of love

there is a beach in Iceland where a great wave rises unexpectedly
and sweeps away all in its path

study the depths attentively
nothing can prepare you for what is to follow

there are more forms of life on our skin
than there are people on earth
2/3 of the planet's inhabitants have never seen snow
in America there are more empty houses
than homeless people
the inhabitants of my settlements caress me like you'd scratch
the cell's wall before execution day

Translated by Andreea Iulia Scridon

The dance of the 7 veils

i haven't blinked for 7 days
i close my eyes one after the other with my left and then right hand
for 7 days now i've had my hands tied over my head
hanging over the lake that is 80 meters deep
children latch on to my hips and legs
and laugh
there are no rollercoasters or fireworks

if love was no more than a chemical reaction
in these four years in which all the cells in my body changed out
i would have been able to forget
i am living proof that love is a little alien
with a brass whistle at its neck
my heart is a juice box with the straw attached

what i say now i won't repeat
because in general i am
a sincere woman
i possess absolute control over lives and changes
it's scary how i manage to keep my calm
the crocodiles lie patient with their heads in the water
i see nothing and hear nothing
i am the master of the crocodiles of these waters
my name is carmen
that was what was said to me — my name was carmen
and i believed him and understood
that once every 7 years i would have to change my name
on the bottom of the lake very fat women put their skins to dry
they paste healing mud onto their bodies

there's so much life here
we're alive and waiting

Translated by Andreea Iulia Scridon

The garden in ruins

we dig for worms in the earth we hang worms on hooks
the greenish liquid trickles down towards the wrist
grandpa says pull hard don't let the fish get away
he said when you grow up only this fish will accompany you
to the very end and it will be exhaustion hopeless and ennui
that you will bury in the place of worms

here at the end of youth far from all the things that i
wanted for myself the feeling that you can get over everything don't be afraid to give
    the earth what it asks of you through the hook
through the eye of the animal that peeks its head out now
and then to sniff the air here is the man who tells you that you are
beautiful and then sheds himself of his old skin

in this village the fear of foxes is greater than the fear of death
the white dog lies at my feet he tells me that no forgetting
can cure this disease come i know a garden in ruins
i'm a good friend of its phantoms i know everything of what's to come
but i don't want to find the end of youth here
i wrap myself up in the shed skin in the middle of the road
come to my subterraneous cities here fears are skyscrapers.

Translated by Andreea Iulia Scridon

Dumitru Fanfarov

the military-industrial complex

the light goes off non-stop and this silence stinks
of another military exercise I wait patiently concentrated
with my notebook on my knees gunpowder sprinkled on the lotus

there's talk of new forms of bunting in the quiet breaks
let them leave so I can ask you:
does the world need to be won over?

proprietors' polygamy tasting of rage and iron
the sky's rest
a new man
the iron's fresh
a pastel
hammock
I swing the stars
as you wouldn't give
chains slaps

this junky little road heading towards nowhere
goals cheap plans cost me too much
for the sake of shortcoming I establish destinations
through muds and swamps shrapnel and splinters
steps fall enlisted into a pair of boots

borrowed from a loan shark

who beats the end of his knout on his thigh waiting for me

caesar gives caesar takes more and more

just like

panoramas that see each other

on strategic roads

god is long out of the picture suffice to say

this is antiphilosophy at the jail's corner

metaphors cease to be

when you least expect it

marks on the boomerang

be careful what you write

where are you my atemporal generation

inside anarchy looks for its discipline outside

I'm writing I hear knocking on the door like the fist of a commandant

like the fist of an office director looking for slaves

like the fist of an Orthodox and secret police priest

same o, same o, all of them wearing the same hat

they come into my house

and tell me I'm under arrest

Translated by Andreea Iulia Scridon

novecento

big cities of course
in which they can wear their bodies
like *a form of love's continuity in space*

everything begins as in an *ancient* film of an old
surrealist love
in which the protagonists devour each other's bodies
athletic and cancerous
alchemically transferring them into the everlasting
till death do us part
is written on the scarves they wear on their eyes
pitch whiteness dribbled with blood of both sexes
like grandma Valentina's first nuptial night
in which she carved her cunt with a knife to be believed

and I believe you when you tell me
and you believe me when I tell you

because love is a voice in unison
which rises up from down there
love is a ventriloquist saint
like the greenish aureole with nipple
like a sea demon with vulva wings
glides over, singing on mount venus
preaching speechless the embodied word
hormonal confessional convulsive
in his hand with a circum*scribe*d member

molecular disquiet bites us tirelessly
in all of heaven there comes an autumn spreading lovers
like leaves which dry out
just the eternal unrepentant and insane swimmers
just the travelers of the forest of nerves

which got to the strip of the sulfur flower
only those who have seen the desert blowing through their ribs
and dreamed of something more
only they will know the vital and internal latch
only they will know how to exit the pattern

Translated by Andreea Iulia Scridon

the light isolator

to be or not to be there is a pinky
I leave the shirking lab
turn up the bass though

invisible people invisible people
until manna rains from the sky again and you see them all
outside walking their electrolytes
useless pulsating short-circuit
with shaggy cats and fingers in the outlet
the pianists slam their keys into me
about boycott and extinction

because I'm just a useless shadow on the earth dear you keep saying
but we're baked and there's no shadow to be seen
because I'm just a useless shadow on the earth dear you keep saying
I'm a light isolator get it through your head
phosphorescent albinos come from copper forms
from among the dead how dead can I be please tell me

just put to sleep the drunk pick-up cunt
your party is filled with idiot mannequins

I am a silver wreck dusk and blizzard in the rearview mirrors
love is in the windows with all the lights on it
I put on the midnight sunglasses
press on the pedal to return home

Translated by Andreea Iulia Scridon

Teodor Dună

cold

the north pole has been pasted to the south pole and both moved to kirilă. he feels
the cold of three winters one on top of each other. he trembles as if shaken by ep-
ilepsy. his small moves fissure the pyramids of spaces and the deltas of times. and
only because he breathes

does a bus flip over in an intersection, its travelers emerge from the windows, howl-
ing, running on sidewalks nodding as if wagging tails, slide on the cold that has
come out of kirilă, the municipality appear suddenly, spreads salt on the streets
around, over the mouths of travelers, mouths full of salt begin to bite, the taste of
flesh awakens ancestral melancholy, teeth become nails, the municipality retreats
like a decimated army, the intersection fills with asphalt walruses, with pieces of
ice, those who were travelers are now eskimos, they make igloos, dig holes, a
floating iceberg comes closer like a huge zeppelin, the antennas on blocks crash
down, massive ads crash down, the iceberg descends spinning towards the inter-
section, the municipality announces the extinction of life to be unacceptable, the
former travelers are surprised to find bouquets of arctic flowers in their hands,
suddenly, all the cold begins to return to kirilă, the carpet of ice is pulled out
from under the feet of former travelers, they all fall like bowling pins, the ads
bleed, the iceberg heads towards kirilă, shrinks, enters through the window, sits
on his chest, makes its way through the skin and kirilă doesn't tremble anymore,
just smiles vaguely towards this birth of quiet. only his heart has remained cold.
as if it were the whole of antarctica in the place of a heart, folded millions of
times, like a closed fist.

Translated by Andreea Iulia Scridon

the happiness marker

kirilă accompanies the walls in their short, silent walks.
he is sorry that they grow tired so quickly and that they don't want to leave
the house. he would very much like to ride the subway surrounded by his
herd of cement elephants.

they are his good friends. because they are always together, because they don't make
    kirilă go away after he strokes them, because they don't scold him when he's just
    a
barefoot childhood with a mouth full of ribbons. he would have wanted the walls to
    be his ivory family. and because they're so gentle, he washes them every Sunday,
    sprays a few drops of perfume on their corners, he takes them in his arms.

sometimes, they smile at him and a crack appears in the plaster. then, kirilă quickly
    draws a wrinkle with a marker. on the cheek, next to the mouth. he can't be dif-
    ferent from his ivory family. he likes to have smile lines very much. he heard that
    it's worth living just to get these wrinkles.

with these kind of wrinkles on his face, kirilă thinks he might be as happy as a wall
    one day.

Translated by Andreea Iulia Scridon

the peripheral circulation of objects

kirilă is tired of kirilă. he sits still on the chair. he counts his fingers with an absent-
    minded air. he doesn't have a single though that belongs to him. so he thinks

of the infernal memory of things that did not happen,
of the fact that his collapse creates a new abyss,
of the system of pre-established harmony,
of the natural precincts of silence,
of the eruption of the most cynical chaos in the divine geometries
of the body,
of the peripheral circulation of objects,
of the fact that it's absurd that the dead are nowhere and that
it's impossible for them not to be somewhere.

kirilă's thoughts blend painfully, he stares at the ceiling
to calm himself and to see. instead of bulbs, more and more
heads of kirilă's, pasted together, leaking into each other,
dripping like atropine directly into his eyes. his irises roll
around, they break a mug, then pulverise the walls. they
split a train full of uranium like two apocalyptic discs.

(because the sum of movement is in continuous descent
in the universe, kirilă wanders from the ashtray to a postcard
of niagara, hitting the walls slowly — this is how he participates
in the postponement of the disappearance.)

Translated by Andreea Iulia Scridon

Cătălina Stanislav

Flemish

I walk past Rembrandt's house today and I want to think something nostalgic
for instance: those green shutters remind me of your eyes
or, oh, remember when we had hot chocolate in that corner café
which is a Dutch bistro now?
What on earth could you buy in a Dutch bistro?
But your eyes are not green
and we never had hot chocolate.
I remember Rembrandt's narrow bed
and this woman Saskia he claimed to love
how strange that my thoughts of you and me back then,
our narrow bed, my wish to be the Saskia
to your boring Flemish painter,
are things that I know I will never think about with other men
And is it weird that I want to tell you what I think about with other men?
Is it weird that I heard a British poet reading today and his hands,
arms,
bony legs and joints that didn't fit quite right,
like Ikea furniture when you skip a step,
his standoffish kind of impatient posture
his big shoes
reminded me of you.
I looked at his belt buckle
and further down
trying to imagine the shape of his penis
and I wanted to tell you about it.

Translated by Marina Sofia

Do you even like Golden Retrievers?

I'd really like to drive around with you right now. The dark roads in this small box of a town wind down beautifully at times, and the radio always plays the same songs. I've told you about that game we used to play when I was small. You'd ask a question, then switch radio stations and the first verse you heard next would answer your question. Sure, sometimes you ask 'will I ever feel whole again?' and the answer is 'it's such a pity you already have yuh wife'. It doesn't always work. That's silly, you say. I asked if we were still in love and I couldn't understand what the guy was singing. Not a single word. I had coffee with a friend at a gas station in Bucharest and I thought about every time the shower curtain falls and it's my fault, every time I'm not with you and it's my fault, every time I am with you and it's my fault. How I'd joke that my CV will say *your girlfriend* underneath occupation and you'd get mad and I'd tell you it's okay, I love you, there's nowhere in the world I'd rather be. There's nowhere in the world I'd rather work. Too soon maybe. If you wanted to ride with me, we would take the same path we always do, the trees would stand guard along the winding road, there'd be no lamp posts, no reaction to our noisy breathing, no words exchanged between us. On the right there's the bike lane where my father's friend fell, and they had to cut off part of his skull and put it in his belly to keep it vascularized. No one believes me when I tell that story. I'm not even sure I remember it correctly now. Once I saw a lost Golden Retriever and you said, he must be close to home, he'll find his way. But I panicked, I made you turn back, search for him, he came to the car, his mouth wide open, blinking in confusion. I reached out to him, but you made a sound, as if you were afraid he'd hurt me. Your fears amplify my own. I tried to find a snack in the back to give him, but when I turned round he had disappeared. I was hoping you would tell me: *I love how caring you are.* And then I looked at you and you said it, and I hated it.

Translated by Marina Sofia

Agree disagree find out

Funny how I place my okcupid app right at the end of my apps list so no one could
    see it
but then it pops up in my Siri suggestions
and I have no idea how to deactivate it.
I find them stupid these people-shopping apps.
yet am pathetic enough to imagine we can measure our compatibility
in smileys, frownies or purple crystal balls which could never save our lives.
What describes your political beliefs Liberal/left in Zara shoes?
Are you a morning person? You should know I will want to have sex with you in the
    morning
but I have a hard time expressing it
Do you believe in the power of prayer? No, but I sometimes do little crosses on the
    roof of my mouth when I slip and fall down the stairs

Translated by Marina Sofia

Seasoning

The pressure I feel when I have to season food
the right way
is somewhat similar to the pressure I feel
to not be the way I usually am
like when someone told me
hey, you didn't seem so high-maintenance
that one time we had sex
or
hey, had fun on that first date, let's go out again
and my fingers freeze on the pink wallpaper of my whatsapp
but then I'm always hyper aware of my salt problem
so I end up putting too much salt
He will soon find out
that I knock over lamps and flowerpots when I'm told to be quiet
or will do painful things like
a kick in the nuts during lengthy foreplay
or tell you I fucking hate you
because I'm jumpy
or maybe because it's true
because I ruin things not when I try too hard
but if I try only a little bit
and he will know that
not only do I use three shower gels, one for each part of my body
all the same brand
I even have a special one when traveling
and somehow that's the most terrifying thing about me.

Translated by Marina Sofia

We'll be fine

I really want to see your lifetime of photos
your girlfriends
your big hair casting a shadow
on the sand beside some ruins you once visited
your hand-me-down winter pullover
hours spent watching TV
together with your parents
your face when you opened the presents
or when your mother woke you up for school
I am irritable in the morning, I bet you are docile and sluggish
like a freshly neutered pet
your face when there's no milk in the fridge
for your coffee
when there is no hope left
in your sad and doubtful eyes
so that I can tell you it's alright
we'll be fine
you'll see just how fine
because if I'm being honest
I never get to tell anyone that
it's ok, we'll be fine
because that is what I always need to hear.

Translated by Marina Sofia

50 ways to leave me or any other girl

Ironically enough my favorite short story in the world is called
How to Be the Other Woman
a sort of instruction manual
for sad second choices
but it never taught me what to do
when it's been confirmed
that you are unworthy of love
this winter
every winter
you are unworthy even of
sitting on the couch next to each other,
to be honest
this crammed apartment holds
every exhausting life-sucking fight
inside its white walls
I have no curtains and the windows
seem to still reflect our sloppy little
silhouettes sharing a kitchen chair
but then again you always complained
that I don't know how to share a chair
I'm greedy in material goods
greedy in space
greedy in love
I want you all to myself
all winter long.
It gets very quiet here at night
I miss going out to smoke on the balcony
it was me and the husbands in the building
blowing out smoke locked on the balcony
from the inside
looking at each other, the little sparks
at the tips of the cigarettes
getting bigger and bigger.

I wanted to nod
we are all adulterous adults here fellas.

Translated by Marina Sofia

Only want to see u holding purple rice

I like to open my blinds at night
the light helps me wake up lighter in the morning
I like to imagine lots of things at times like these
when we all complain of loneliness and fear,
poor health, fleeting lives and cold feet in the morning
I imagine a gray city that I've never seen in real life
maybe only in films or on TV
or a Christmas poem
and I imagine you in front of some large windows
with light streaming in
you ask me something casual
like: hey, did you open this bag of rice?

Just like I dreamt once that you asked me
about a purple bag of rice I had in the kitchen
as if we knew each other well
as if we'd bought that bag together
as if you wanted basmati while I preferred the sticky kind
so we compromised and bought the sticky kind
and you held my hand at the store
like we cooked that rice together
I dropped in too much salt
and you told me it was good
but you lied.
It's so hard to be good at being lonely
but I'm an ambitious girl
Eventually I become good at everything.

Translated by Marina Sofia

Ana Donțu

god spent a few hours in the mall
watching people succeeding each other
on the escalators

Translated by Andreea Iulia Scridon

all the silence

gathered in six hours
dissipates
the morning brings my thoughts
back to flesh that no longer invites me in
it pours out of the bed horrified
and with its hands trembling on the lid
it throws me out
no morning air
can clear my imagination —
the crown of the head opens with supermarket backs
from which the surrogates of happiness pop out
with them I fill my nights
something moves in the plexus
it crawls onto my neck
it opens my head
like a window that looks towards a wall

Translated by Andreea Iulia Scridon

love poem

I made coffee
and forgetting, I poured it
in two cups

Translated by Andreea Iulia Scridon

there's not enough darkness anymore
for me to feel like I'm in my comfort sone
with the window open
I try not to make a sound
although I'm home alone
the feeling of nausea
covered by a cigarette
the tremor of the hands
the dizziness that drowns images in smoke
I stay like this because it passes
I never ask myself
about the things I do
everything is somehow
random

Translated by Andreea Iulia Scridon

Robert Gabriel Elekes

after I correct my translations
after I grab my meal tickets
after I take the 28 bus home
and take care not touch anyone else
after I buy canned fish from the supermarket
after I watch
the last episode of the walking dead,
then I'll accept her friend request.

Translated by Andreea Iulia Scridon

the portrait of the protestor as a young man

I stand in the rain at protests and gaze into the void with boredom,
damn, how simple and natural
this thing looked on radu vancu's facebook page.
even if I want change, I don't really feel like jumping
or yelling at an empty building
or at those who didn't come out on the streets
I don't find it too healthy
so I gaze into the void with boredom and resist
I try to keep agoraphobia and misanthropy at bay
thinking of the fact that one day I'd like to fall in love
with a hoodlum with ovaries,
a no-nonsense girl, a Valkyrie from oltenia
who would put me in my place.
that I'd like to start a rock band in my garage
and we would only perform in apartment block basements.
that I'd like to someone to film how the bellybutton lint
gathers, I find this a very tender moment.
that at 33 years old I should give up so many bad habits
that there's not a lot of time left to learn new things.
that there are days when I'd just like to fly somewhere,
not to get away, just to get patted down at security,
or I could go dancing in the security and pat someone down myself,
and that the me-too-ists would say that the first kid
is louis c.k. type harassment and the second is the harvey weinstein type.
that the cat has more food in the fridge than me.
that I won't survive longer than the reality tv show entitled survivor.
that my tamagotchi which croaked
before my eyes 23 years ago
might have been my first and last offspring.

Translated by Andreea Iulia Scridon

post-confessionalism

I believe that the future literary historians will be
password hackers and data miners
the coolest ones will be those who find the music
that I listened to on last.fm, who or what I photographed
on instagram, what rhymes I looked up on
rimeaza.ro, with what poet friends I chatted on
messenger, what books I read on
goodreads, what rando I screwed on
tinder, what new words of hungarian I learned on
dex.ro, what porn I masturbated to by searching my
chrome history, and what films and games I downloaded
and which writers I plagiarized
on facebook, what cringe bombs I posted on
my email, what responsibilities I ignored
while writing this poetry book.

By that time,
I wonder how much cryptocurrency my poetry will be worth?
I wonder if
stepping in my virtual footprints
they'll don my virtual flesh
and roll in the hay of my virtual life
and will they become posthuman intellectual pigs-in-a-blanket?

Translated by Andreea Iulia Scridon

Anastasia Gavrilovici

what I'm up to

for Maria

from radiation the hair on the hands stopped growing the blood has certain aromas
natural identical to petrol to rust and at home we eat
fast-food each other you have already learned
the weak points the places where god forgot his little shovels
buried in little mounds of cancer the expiration date of
the happy gland and how you could bear it in April
when on the screen two little girls with shaved heads hold out a massive
burdock leaf you smile
with this little umbrella stuck inside your brain under which a grenade hisses already
    you smile
to the beggar who showed up a few years ago the chaotic movements of a polish
    dance
before he disappeared with his Pegas-brand bicycle
under the wheels of a truck

i'd write you about the nights in which the chairlift cables enter
and leave my mouth in the hopes that my phobia of long hair still
makes you laugh taking pictures of my congested faces and
bungee jumping over my mind have remained
the little pleasures you still allow yourself

now i've finally understood. the dolphins trained for military missions
push you with their snouts towards the shore the organ deposits are open round the
    clock any
coat has a built-in parachute you can try anything there's no way
to get out of this mess

still you can lift the curtain take a peek at the correct and demented show
don't turn your head just lift the veils from my face wrinkled
from so much laughter for you I let them fill up my cortex
with granules for you the compulsive clanking and gestures of a man with
peter pan syndrome someday I'll grow
baseball bats instead of legs I'll
get to the end of it all.
no reason for you to worry.

Translated by Andreea Iulia Scridon

The lives of others

I read about the lives of others on Wikipedia,
about Sven Marquardt, the bouncer from Berghain who wouldn't let people
into the club if he didn't like their face, about Saint Anastasia the Great Martyr,
deliverer of poison and about the final heir and cat
of Karl Lagerfeld. If someone tried to tell the story of my life
on Wikipedia they would have no difficulty in doing so.
I'm not even 24, but it has something of the rhythm and clarity of an IV drip.
The minute and great pleasures, emotional nuances, things that tear my heart
to shreds sit lined up and sparkle alluringly, like multicolored
pieces of sushi in a box invaded by ants. I have only ever loved
one man, who now turns towards me when he can't find his words,
and that makes me happy. When he isn't around, I feel a dull
sadness, like when you tried for 3 months to put plastic with plastic,
glass with glass, paper with paper and here comes the garbage truck
and dumps them all together. My child, now the size of a bean,
meets the other beans from the salad eaten at lunch.
They contain fibers, magnesium, essential neurotransmitters for memory,
exact terminology, couriers of contentment.
I'm still young, fertile, patient, a bush
of fumewort whose flowers will last for a long time,
that is, if the city's dogs won't come over to relieve themselves anytime soon.
Outside the autumn begins, an autumn as unequivocal and predicable as
a literary critic from Cluj, I'm ready for anything and don't give a shit
if my mug wouldn't let me into the most hardcore
club in Berlin.
If someone wants to tell the story of my life
on Wikipedia, I'd like them to remember one fact:
the way in which we hold hands in our sleep, like otters in water
in order to not be carried by the current
away from each other.

Translated by Andreea Iulia Scridon

What do you know about hunger, mister Patrimony?

As things are seen from on high, as from on down we don't understand anything
someone wrote when sharing an image of a police drone
with Notre Dame in flames. At 22:05, when the fire is still eating
away at the roof, many viewers are already thinking
of the artistic potential of these iconic images.
A tired playwright gone to live in France says that the tragic fire
forces us to ask ourselves profound questions about the use of drama.
Of course we must. A simple scroll shows us that, on the same day, a
child was found dead in the school's septic tank, but the child isn't
important, it had just a 3 year history, not one of 850 years.
The amazonian forest doesn't all burn at once,
but bit by bit, though controlled fires.
When fire scorched the house of a family with 8 children, nobody
reduplicated that banal construction,
Because a house is not a national symbol or one of European civilization.
It's not important.

      ***

When grandma's barn burned down with everything inside it, in the summer in
    which
she was widowed for a second time, it wasn't important, that barn didn't
have
rosettes or lacy facades. No emperor was crowned inside of it,
though a few calves were born. When the nursing home in
Focşani burned down it wasn't important, because it wasn't
visited by 14 million tourists a year.
No money. No profit. No 5 euro
postcards. No picture for instagram. When my mole was
cauterized it wasn't important, though it was swarthy and
gothic, but my mole isn't a tourist objective, my mole
isn't included in the patrimony.

      ***

What do you know about hunger, mister Patrimony?
About raped women, who have no bracelets but those made from
salami rinds? Who have known only the makeup of bruises?
About exploded Syrians, human rubble and death in the flower of life?
About the intubated faces that disappear behind automatic doors
forever?
About poverty and misery and drinkable water?
That's how things look from on down, since from on high you can't understand
    much.
But don't be sad, mister Patrimony, anyway we want
hospitals, not cathedrals, anyway we have Versailles and
the Sixtine Chapel, the Eiffel Tower and the Sagrada Familia,
Manneken Pis and Champs-Elysées.
You are an aesthetic eclipse of a dizzying perversity, a constellation
of magnets on the refrigerators of intellectuals. A summer drizzle
which neither helps nor ruins things.
You are a cactus which doesn't need anything.
Teach me, now more than ever,
how to be like you.

Translated by Andreea Iulia Scridon

Natural Born Digitals

As I stand near the subway doors, with
my shopping bags, grave and pregnant, I look at people
sitting down, at the heads plunged into phone screens, with
that grief with which I gazed only at the
boy I liked in high school when I found
out that he was gay. A yuppie decked out in Zara and Massimo Dutti
watches videos with a Chinese guy repairing chipped vases using
ground-up instant noodles, transformed into a solid paste with the force
of chemicals. She's having brutal revelations, her pupils dilate, I can feel
that she'll give it a like.

Last night I saw a movie in which, every time the two
had a fight, she cooked an omelet for him with toxic mushrooms,
provoking within him a terrible indigestion, which made him more
vulnerable than a ficus
in periods of renovation, more helpless than a deaf-and-dumb
trinket seller robbed by two kids with ADHD. Then he implored her
to stay, to take care of him and everything would turn out well. Some
would call this love, my contemporaries would name it postirony or
post-sincerity, cultural options which don't impress me. We are
sanguine buffoons, hyper-digitalized and unprepared for life, just
numbers in statistics held by wide napes and ladies from whom
language is a curl blocked between two scorching hair rollers.
We need sun, tanning lotion, dull little jokes from Times New Roman
newspaper. We need sex. We need Xanax. We are answers.

Translated by Andreea Iulia Scridon

Questionnaire

Attention! For the improvement of the quality of the services offered by our organization, this conversation will be recorded. After the beep, please press the # key and answer firmly.

Describe yourself in ten words. Be careful what you choose, words create images, and the images might affect the emotions of those around you.
What do you like most about yourself? What do you hate most about yourself? Who are you when nobody's looking at you, who shaves you in the places you can't reach?
We don't want to know what you'll be when you grow up, just tell us
if you got your first job long after your first
blow job and describe in short any of the ticked experiences.
Mention three European values with which you resonate and for which
you would be willing to commit seppuku in the parking lot of the biggest mall
in your city. Why do you think you should be selected to participate in this International
festival
for talented people under the age of 25 that have no idea how
to open a tightly sealed jar
who never made sports bets and who have no direction in life?
Life on Mars, life in the countryside, a country as good as any other, list the proposed
options in accordance with your personal preferences.
What was your most recent charitable act? When did you
last get involved in the life of your community? Do you believe that women,
homosexuals and
pretzel braiders enjoy the same rights as you do and
that together you form the heart of society?
Define the word heart.
Define it one more time and compare your responses with those of your neighbors
or with
the correct answers at the end.
In what country would you never want to live?

In what country would you have preferred to be born?

Do you think that if there were more tobacco plantations in Europe,

children should be sent to work on them? Do you consider yourself a moral person?

Describe your last erotic dream in a few phrases.

If you could live in a film, which would it be? Convince us in 5 lines.

Do you believe the world would be a better place without you?

What is your contribution to improving quality of life? Or birth rates?

Do you prefer vertical or horizontal graves? Incineration or inhumation?

Spicy or sweet ketchup?

Are you somebody who has double standards?

What talents or abilities would you most like to have?

Do you believe that masturbation, just like poetry, is the affair of

lonely misfits?

How long are you willing to wait to keep your place in line

for your call to be answered? Are you the kind of person

who prefers to see their name on books instead of meal vouchers?

Tell us what discounts you're entitled to so that we can tell you who you are.

Tell us that you don't care about money, but about experience, admit that you too

are here for the Prosecco afterwards, tell us that you and anal, never,

you and lies, never, and you and subterfuges hailing luck and fame, never,

since you don't want any of this, only to *make the world a better place.*

Do you believe with all your heart that beauty will save the world?

Or at least the European Union?

Answer the above questions honestly, leave us an email

address

and you will be contacted with your results

by one of our operators

as soon as possible.

Translated by Andreea Iulia Scridon

Andrei Dósa

My parents' things

Until mom and dad come back from work I have time to look inside mom's nightstand. In dad's I found green boxes, decorated with butterflies. There aren't butterflies inside, just balloons. Balloons work too. They're hard to blow up and slip away. I'm going to tie them to the corners of the house. But only when all three of us are at home. Or when my parents fight, without realizing it. My dad also has a compass in his drawer. I open its lid and instead of an N there's an M engraved on. The compass will always point towards mom. This way we surely won't get lost. Inside mom's nightstand I find a blue box full of white submarine-shaped pills. On the aluminum foil there's a calendar. I'll talk to mom. Secretly, mom and I give dad a pill each day. After dad swallows it, the pill becomes a submarine, and mom can see inside dad through a periscope. We'll check why he is upset. At the bottom of the drawer is a black, shiny box. Divided in small squares, like a computer but labeled with colors instead of numbers.   Mom doesn't know how to multiply the colors for one to be happy. Nor does she know how one should read the solution in the mirror that is on the other side of the box. Mom does not use the black box anymore. Dad is very good at math. But we will take care of all these, while our house, lifted up by dad's balloons, will float over the cities, and people will smile at us and wave. Look, a happy family, they'll say.

Translated by Andreea Iulia Scridon

Someone had a little note on which it was written that I am the king's son (on my way home)

someone was locked inside me
caspar hauser was locked in
a room full of mirrors
if I let him out now
people would be scared of him
they wouldn't know how to hide anything
he would try to read people's faces
like he used to read his own face in the mirror
and would feel alone, terribly alone

Translated by Andreea Iulia Scridon

and her blonde peach fuzz

after three months
of washing dishes
around me now spins
the Bronx shaman
with his trumpet
I lie down on the bench
I smile
the sky reflects
in my sunglasses
seagulls glide
carried by currents
the statue of liberty
lets out a naked foot
just for me
and her blonde peach fuzz

Translated by Andreea Iulia Scridon

request

this must be
love:
someone who wants
to start it all over again
even on your behalf

Translated by Andreea Iulia Scridon

assistance

someone has to be there to help
the kids on roller-skates
when they want to go up the stairs
and always be there for them
sometimes people need help
when happiness ends

Translated by Andreea Iulia Scridon

non-coherences/descending moves

on the tin rooftops
the felines flaunt their bodies
charged with static energy
over the city the sky stirs nothing, moves nothing
despite atmospheric pressures and accumulations of vapors
yellow taxis are ready quick to jump in
and show everyone the Balkanic art of exaggeration
bugs fall on their backs
and bat their antennae like a uni-lash

still in a strange way
the possibility of defining the logic of the days flutters
sometimes through my synapses
under the form of a physics equation
the vizier asks
how fast the mufti's son must run
while holding several ice cubes in his hand
so that they don't melt
before he serves them to his master

if god had a face- and sometimes he does
I'd follow the movement of his lips and the way
he gesticulates pointing expertly towards architectural sections of the edifice
where they produce Guy Fawkes masks
issuing statistical data for further efficiency

sometimes it's easy for me to talk to god
because both of us are incoherent
because both of us are westerners

Translated by Andreea Iulia Scridon

ridiculous and beautiful

I used so much community discipline
for desire for the climax of wellbeing
I whipped my body I sacrificed
all resources on dopamine

free now that nobody sees me
I perceive my gestures as theatrical

generally my friend
we freak out with pleasure when we receive appreciation
when I choose to treat you
like the real golden boy
I therapize myself into happiness and then
a tear trembles in the corner of the eye
athletes with medals in bunches at the necks
lined up at the starting line
and enthusiastic journalists
we go home and we write about ourselves

it's both ridiculous and beautiful
Contorted facial muscles
the laugh reflected in smoky double-gaze
so gregarious so barbarous

it's both ridiculous and beautiful
it's a media catastrophe

Translated by Andreea Iulia Scridon

pathetic atrocities

there is no refuge for the rejected
there is no court of law in which they could plea
their case
there is only the tide movement
of pain in the chest and self-pity

her image in stone and unjust words
resounding over the waves
which slowly destroy

I have thought pathetic atrocities
for my suffering to pass faster
the tears of a unicorn gone through hell
reappearing in the corner of the eye
like a drop of cyanide

Translated by Andreea Iulia Scridon

Claudiu Komartin

A Matter of Perspective

We wake up before sunrise,
A good meal in the morning, cereal, coffee with milk
and a sustained effort of willpower not to give up.
Towards lunch we all start to hiccup
(on the other side they certainly talk about us again
on the other side they don't give a damn about awkward alibis
that we thought would save us from whatever would come.)

Visits are allowed to those in quarantine
although there's enough space for the usual
excuses and guilt trips of the innocents who
still try to abide despite all that we've seen.
Of course, you can also be armored by N95 masks and by carrying
forged health declarations —
it's a question of sincerity that they ask themselves,
all who smile at each other lost among the cars stopped
behind the barrier.

It'll be a long time until the barrier rises,
I hope you've gathered serious provisions
as you expect the next epidemics
and that you know what to do to control panic.

The day is almost equal to night,
ethically speaking we can also perceive reality with our eyes closed.
Everything is a question of perspective, my girlfriend says.
My girlfriend wears a wine-colored kimono and cuts through
the lungs of the best prepared candidates.

Translated by Andreea Iulia Scridon

Mbl

A touch of madness in the air, a semitone lower
than progressive brutalization of a species hangs
unhoped once more.

Numerical idolatry has arrived and it is not going anywhere anytime soon,
temples shall be erected in its honor,
altars of silicone monitored by cyber-archangels and trans-seraphs,
from where the great priests will preach about the uses
and glory of herd immunity.

Directors giving edicts, the genius of the masses with its frightened
science of transience.

So many people crushed trying to protect
what they did not know how to love at the right time.

We would have sworn on biochemistry. On nuclear physics. On nanobots.

From tender and gullible bluebells we've turned
into sickly dahlias.

Only in poems everything is endless,
save for silence.

Translated by Andreea Iulia Scridon

allegory

my head feels veiled, and my heart is rowing against the current.
last night I dreamt of a god holding a little key,
lost among the ruins of Kaliacra.
groups of tourists with almond-shaped eyes passed by him,
or quite through him, neglecting him.

he was, it's true, a tiny little god,
negligible,
almost as negligible as a shrimp
while dozens of white orcas slammed against the shore,
forcefully,
challenging his stillness.
mean. spiteful. fattened beyond measure.

(what were those orcas doing in the sea with the most negligible supplies
for immanence? what was I doing there,
in the decrepit hour of dusk, when nobody has any power left
except to follow the waves
in a procession of filial mourning?

my face came loose from my body, it floated dozing
and stuck itself on the little key, like a dirty, ragged carcass
for the times in which people feel only the nape of their necks
and nowhere else.

I woke up with my ears ringing
I woke up with the urge to go reach
the lonely and shrunken god
and turn his little key on
or maybe just hide him from everyone and everything,
In the drawer where dad used to keep his belt
and his decorations.

Translated by Andreea Iulia Scridon

Epigrams

writing doesn't help anyone, you were right again, mom

glory doesn't help anyone, much less you, old man
who no longer fit into your skin from so many prizes and tumors

lawsuits don't help anyone, or you, the innocents who didn't suspect
anything up to the fatal moment when all sorry whores of your country
write how they were sobbing for three weeks straight

lanterns don't help, darkness is enough

what you thought you knew does not help, all the strings have been cut
and now you float aimlessly, waiting for all things everything to become
clear and definitive

militancy does not help, be those occupants of cafés
on the left bank of self-destruction

drowning your sorrow is ridiculous when being sorry is the food
they fed you with and they never told you that there was also

another way of living, that life can be lived beyond their twisted
laws, by counterfeit guarantees of a socially "successful career"

that mountain of trash where you bathe hoping for self-oblivion and attrition
doesn't help anything either,
reports and statistics do not help, isn't that clear?

Ivan Patzaichin's broken oar is the only proof that
an oar can break when you need it most

drugs do not help, unless you get them from the right person

"obtaining what is universal through what is axiomatic" is a stupid quote
for intellectual creeps!

hospitals are just the Russian roulette that you play
blindfolded like poor Fyodor before a sarcastic
and precise execution squad

trusting you helps me with nothing it helps movies about outlaws

we swim livid and scatterbrained in the great economic depression,
in Wallachia even the dust turns to dust

Translated by Andreea Iulia Scridon

Reactionary elegies

For Mr. Dușan Petrovici†

1.

saturated hydrocarbons steroids pesticides
boundless influxes of money and disregard
all that we experience defies the few years in which it seemed
that there is peace down under they insinuated
poisons the art of the bubonic and voracious slam dunk

from the seed of man now something is extracted
more rotten than the great and toxic sea
of a generation and some
do you remember — the little
goldfish had suffocated in a clear bag
thrown directly on the sidewalk, his revenge will be
the kilo of plastic removed from your guts after
the feast of oysters and calamari we are
tired pianos caught in the hauberk net
bloated in our depraved happiness we row
dressed in tuxedos towards the island where
radioactive people flourish doxa
replaced with noxa trapped consciences
by lust someone invokes the toy of the last innocents

and the lilies catch fire

2.

it burns and it hurts and the bottles
are quite empty in this time morgan
freeman sleeps
he has no idea that at the gates of the orient people
slap each other even in their sleep and

the country's idiots are named your eminency
sir

psychosis as a form of integration with agrarian ideals
odometers with meters under pillows under asses
and tuberose perfumes look,
great emperor, we invented
digital mosquitoes and gadflies
beneath our wide open eyes, the corporation produces loads
of Breivik ogres ramified into fractals
and plans the assassination of another archduke

so let the robots come and stamp us
with the seal of calamity
-our double chin saturated with heavy metals will rise again
towards the skies it will spit again towards the stars

     3.

In this sphere of social fragility the sun
reveals its destiny of being an
disconsolate auntie
seeped across the trees' bark it shows us
how happiness must be taken by force snatched brutally
but I'm still waiting in the native perimeter
spying from the mint bushes created to begin to move
the bread that ate half my face off

I use cataplasms, medicinal tea, ointments
homeopathic remedies as prescribed by fairytales-I am
the usurper of melancholy and of my own
dated sentiments tinkering away at an
instrument that will replace thinking
sadness and I live intensely
and urgently the dramas communicated through
oracular capillaries

by people who live their biographies ferociously
and I know well that in these territories all of us
fight to catch the next day
without fanfares or extravaganzas or ivory towers

because it's dog eat dog

Translated by Andreea Iulia Scridon

Merlich Saia

***

I'd like to believe
that there's a room somewhere
where no one demands anything from me
that's where I want to go.
I make a hopscotch of garments,
skip, throw a gem from my earrings,
count out loud, am happy, laugh.
The sun sets and rises and is everywhere.

In front of my room there's another room,
kept locked at all times. No one there expects anything of me.
No one's there. How nice.
Too many people, too many rooms that swallow me up.
So nice, that's where I want to go,
skip and hop.
His drunken body, stark naked,
so beautiful. I want him. I want to gather him up off the floor.
We'll never know each other nor meet nor die.
Haven't even changed my clothes.
The price of regrets – I cannot afford
such behavior. I have to do more,
bear it with pleasure, lose
some of my beauty but that is not
the reason they come to me.

I forgot that this is what I'm paid for. That's why
my body is covered in bruises
it takes a week for them to disappear

I examine each change in pigmentation.
Those bruises look like the dresses I discarded last week
clean
interchangeable
pretty
and ever so slightly
extremely sad.

I'm being eaten alive by my survival strategy.
My body is filled with hundreds of people
who've yet to utter a word.

***

I'm using all the tricks in the book to hide the dead.
I'm hungry and it stinks of food.
I'm so dreadfully hungry. Someone is blithely cooking
at this late hour. I can hear the marinaded meat fizzing in hot oil,
bell peppers, onions, and I don't know anyone
who'd ask me to dinner right now,
nor find an app to identify the food smells, or friends
to eat with at this time of night.
The woman made of sand lies sleeping, the man made of sand lies awake.

All my stuff stayed in that room,
they're all there, in order: boxes with clothes,
boxes with toys, boxes with pictures of me,
pictures without me, above all, pictures without any other people.

You can find them all here. The clothes I wore,
the clothes I never wore, the clothes chosen by others
to be liked by others.

Those last should've come with pockets,
deep like Mariana Trench

or some other deepest hole of all.

Would have made it much easier
for me to hide.

***

Today's the day when I first saw sunflower fields in bloom. Blue skies.
All the things I've been part of are only just happening.
Today's the day when I last saw the sunflower fields
floating gently above the ground.
My long hair spread out on the grass
my clothes torn, my lip cut open
a few red veins
thread their way up into the very heart of the anthill.

Here's where the little girl sleeps
dreaming of the city.
Every room in that city is full
of tiny fairy toys in color
the sun rolls from side to side of the chamber

Then
the woman with no clothes on lies down on the bed
white sheets white clouds gestures of love
tumble to the ground
constructing the perfect city

Here and now
I fall into the arms of a soft toy
contemplating the little girl who lies dreaming.
A few stray hairs are caught in her purple hairband.
My body must not be left on its own anymore.

Back then
when I did what I did
I was thinking
of a starlit sky with shooting stars
but all I saw was a starlit sky where all the stars had been shot.

Just a short while ago I was content
to listen to the swish of my dirty laundry
how to measure the distance between us
when you've cut your nails?

I was so beautiful
You were so beautiful
We got used to falling asleep on our own
we no longer mind
we share a body
left out in the corridor
dragging hundreds of kilos of beauty

Translated by Marina Sofia

Olga Ștefan

the parable of the sower

i shall set the stubble field on fire,
the bed in which i sleep,
the woman made of stone
and-, her innocent breast,

just to knock down the great granaries, the souls,
and to dig your sleeping-spot on the mountain's rib.

i saw the future:
it was the crushed snail next to the snail you shelter,
your ear bleeding, the young girl's wet nape,
her bejeweled wrists.

o, god of refusals:
mice exploding with poison.
Still wander out of your mercy
out of your mercy, my soul (which you will claim, in the end)
goes down into the bunker,

and the little and rubicund god
follows it, too.

Translated by Andreea Iulia Scridon

until we meet again in 2017

welcome mrs heatwave, mrs death,
mr future.

as if school weren't over in
two days and the tomatoes from oltenia and rock hard cherries already on the table
you throw your handcuff away, you protect your laziness, the bones laid out,
ordering the world under the prideful flesh of girls
who aren't very pretty

(spandex and cheap lycra, white sandals over nude pantyhose,
young farm girls with space for sexual projections and drama)

in the poem, you splayed yourself over the macadam and the phantom wrinkles its
     breasts
and cape in weeks of taxis

in front of you there is the frugal meal you ate before you get
your monthly check
the linen blend blouse from the corner shop, the cotton skirt,
the quartz pendant, the earrings with dolphins, baby powder.

in the mirror, the dark circles from before you made peace with life
still romantic, the fixed form of banal truth:
the feeling that you're far from being free, that
from the shameful blood in the handkerchief, from the cotton ball
that peaks out
of the anemic's nostrils
from the pointer finger
comes the fervor of a postponed revolution.

Translated by Andreea Iulia Scridon

the girls of the fatherland

malnourished
lolitas
thank their benefactor.

their hemp-colored hair shining with cleanliness.
cords of silk
hold it in its place.

ave,
here we enter your last year on earth.

we waited for the atomic cloud and its dizzying
summer.

the remains of summer boil, the wormy tomatoes in kitchens.

the latter we took, when they were still alive, to the common grave.

together we saluted the sun and the field's burned line.
we returned to singing songs of greatness.
glistening horizons, factories and villages
over which the night falls.

the rally to multiply, urgently, the pure line
of those convicted
cut into volcanic rock,
shall be silenced.
so the gluey disgust of day which melts
into evening.

the girls of the fatherland
did not nestle the instincts of amazons
into the hearts of cows

only in their stomachs, among predatory fish,
landscapes-one upside down and the other inside out and, exhausted,
in sick cocoons, of silk,

slender crochets and
belts of gold.

Translated by Andreea Iulia Scridon

Mina Decu

10.

I won't tell you anything nice
anything clean
or tender
honest
or who knows
nothing
I'm trying to widen my niche
to squeeze through
and disappear
there's always a valve
and this drives you out of your mind
you search
keep searching
a voice
a sound
which

Translated by Andreea Iulia Scridon

14.

I won't say anything about myself here
nothing about viscera
nothing about sclera
nothing about the way I wash
or don't wash
dishes
laundry
or the floors with anyone who would want to get to something this way
that is believed to become through exposure
truer
more of a poem
shit
I don't even have strong words for you
sublime words
concepts
words gone to hell
words that suck the erect cock
of the most perverted pimp
unimagined by any poet
pathetically hammy with its own words
that shoot out like sperm
on the cheeks of a doll named doina
with broken eyes and lips smeared with nail polish
nothing about rain
like an axe directly in the crown of the head
or about the lace dress that I will never
wear
because fuck lace
and nothing about pigs fleas hamsters copper or white
nothing about money
nothing about children
I won't use any exit ramp
and I'll still see from now on

the most beautiful word
when it's uttered with a mouthful of smoke
before a glass of liquor
is shit

Translated by Andreea Iulia Scridon

37.

We search in films in music in paintings on streets in trees I watched the clouds I
wanted to find exactly what I was feeling I needed a mirror something that would
open before me like a pomegranate to see its beauty and recognize my feelings in
every purplish perfect grain that if crushed between my teeth would have left a
sweet and sour aroma in my mouth would have made me feel that I'm alive as if I
were biting out of a heart I didn't dare tell people about this I searched I contin-
ued to search silently clenching my teeth gnashing them on dry land chomping a
murderous bite of stale air a compact stubborn muteness to the sky to the earth
until the very last catch of the wrist I couldn't imagine that I would ever find that
the aroma would finally flood my mouth my pores and my mind but when I sat
there on his right side next to his placental silence the pomegranate unfurled be-
fore me crushed against my lips, seed by seed, the taste color of impartiality full-
ness of beauty escape from the wasteland

Translated by Andreea Iulia Scridon

51.

nothing warms you up anymore
at the seaside with ice at your feet
you think that life can't be any more alive
and you tremble
it doesn't seem at all strange
that you don't see waves
you don't hear seagulls
that everything is smooth and white
that not a single shell
peeks its head out of the snow
just a white expanse as in Russian novels
here
so close
By the border of a country you never visited
last night you drank too much
and wanted to hear the water
but you couldn't
so you left
and shooed him away who was coming up behind you
now not even a dog
silence
silence
and white
no sound
breathe
and you're afraid not to break something
and bend the air with your breath
you're cold
you hug yourself
and smile
thinking of how far away you are

Translated by Andreea Iulia Scridon

Radu Nițescu

song 2.1

in my backyard
in the shed
where I never took you
because it's ugly not for the likes of you

in the shed then
I began to build a ship
the on-board computer has been responding to orders for two days now
the communications are ready
life's maintenance system is ready
and all the other systems and subsystems and the little wheels and nails
are ready

now I'm working on movement through hyperspace
you know, that thing with wormholes, I told you
about it one evening

and when all the wars here will end
what do you say we head towards the farthest star
and see what's up there

just you
and me

Translated by Andreea Iulia Scridon

(images)

an uninterrupted white wall
nibbled by rain
makes the trees far away
different from those in the hospital courtyard

here the noise begins
when men women and children go mute

some wait for a doctor
another waits for salvation
corina waits for her mother who will never come

the god of the many has a sculpted face
he strolls
and begs for cigarettes
when it rains the priest holds sermons

sometimes he says
the farthest of the far away lands is here
tight next to you

Translated by Andreea Iulia Scridon

we all have a pornhub heart

The chitin armour protects the mosquito from scattering
its thorax on the walls and three butterflies spin in the light,
large, clumsy, good only to be left alone,
but she wants to catch them in an empty pickle jar,
and then release them, give them freedom.
Recently, I read that at Ohio State University they
conducted a study on the giant blue butterflies in Peru.
They discovered that the texture of the wings can be reproduced
for high-tech dust and water-resistant carcasses.
And look, bro, how death reaches the Lepidoptera.
Tiny scales remain on her fingers when she covers
the jar and I have a duty to fantasize that some of that will
land on my penis. Then I realize that I'm here,
in the butterfly jar, where joy can
only lose ground.

It's so quiet that you can hear the Coca-Cola in the glass,
constantly, without refrain.

Translated by Andreea Iulia Scridon

i play with the black ball

made of rubber

behind the window
winter
is happening
very slowly

and i play with the black ball
made of rubber

Like a dog that is
home alone

like a human that is
alone in the mind

Translated by Andreea Iulia Scridon

Vlad Dimitriu

yeti doesn't have options

yeti always knows what he wants,
he doesn't need to choose.
That's why we can only come to know yeti
in the wilderness,
where he lives.
Our world isn't good for him,
because in our world you can choose
the way things are done.

Translated by Andreea Iulia Scridon

The family needs to leave society.

The family can't be the pillar of society anymore.
It needs to be sent to the wilderness.
There's enough love for everyone there.

Translated by Andreea Iulia Scridon

Let's work in yeti.

Everyone works
and for this reason things stay put.
We need to leave work
and go to yeti.

Translated by Andreea Iulia Scridon

The moment elapses first

Then things happen.
The distance between the lapse of the moment
and the things that take place within it
is a narrow and poorly lit corridor.
Inside it, the results are posted and inside it you can escape.

Translated by Andreea Iulia Scridon

Once together they don't separate.

You gaze can never fall on
something falling,
your eye can never truly follow
something that falls.
In order to perceive falling things,
you must fall with them.

Translated by Andreea Iulia Scridon

We don't have the gift of flight.

No one can fly
About the earth.
By self-propulsion
We are the only beings that know dance.
This is the most important message
that we transmit to future generations.

Translated by Andreea Iulia Scridon

The human factor

He takes the thing and says something else about it.
He goes far away and from that distance speaks
about the things here until they break.
He doesn't ever stay quiet out of fear of saying something.
He is an engineer, artist, doctor, specialist,
lawyer professor and he has a big and rusty knife
with which he'll cut your neck.
After making a bloodbath of you he'll take your corpse,
photograph it and film it
until it dries up and then give it to TV or
eat it.
His TV eats any sort of guts,
hair or fat.
You can't escape it.
All those who succeed in escaping
from him are like him.
He has a tall factory where people in pajamas
take their things at night
and he gives them numbers in exchange.
They're all afraid
that the numbers won't end after they die.

Translated by Andreea Iulia Scridon

The human factor in the garden

From here Goods and Clarity extend onwards.
He takes them and places them in hands,
sets them one over the other.
In the morning he drinks a coffee and smokes a cigarette.
The goods are identical to each other,
they have nothing in common.
The sun sends rays of light on earth,
they light up the cars
and swings enter through the library's window,
caress animal orchards and wheels.
He hurries down the road,
paying no mind to the end of the road,
On the side all the places he's going to are lined up.
He takes care, eats what's roasted,
gets decked up in them,
decks them up, climbs the stairs,
goes down the stairs,
locks and unlocks cabinets.

Translated by Andreea Iulia Scridon

Cristina Ispas

thephysicalworld

A broken puzzle
and Natalia gazing at it, lost.

I slip a pill under my tongue,
I pull a surgical mask over my mouth
so I don't pass my cold over to her
and I get up from whatever it is I'm doing to help her.

But I probably look terrible,
because you make a sign, saying you'll take over
and I should go out somewhere.

While I'm smoking a cigarette out on the street
after a few weeks
of practically not leaving the house
and even more weeks of not smoking
I look at the cars that stop at the red light
and at the faces of the people in the cars.

I imagine they're coming back from the office
or from shopping
or from hanging out with their friends
that inevitably they're doing more or less the same things
hence their common expression
of vague tightness.

A sort of inconvenience instead of a life
work just for money

joys ticked off the list with a lot of effort behind them.

No one passes on the sidewalk
just the snow that keeps falling quietly.

A tall, thin woman in a short skirt in the frost
stops and makes the sign of the cross in front of the military unit
where, hidden in the dark
there's a small wooden church.

The physical realm in which we try so hard
not to be alone.

In warm overalls with a knitted cap on backwards
some neighbor's little boy keeps busy
on his little yellow planet lit up by the streetlight.

A little ways over, a deep bass overflows
from a car buried in the snow
orbited by a young man holding a shovel.
The boy's father.

In bed, while sipping my tea
waiting for it to fight back the fever
I'm thinking of reading a few more pages
before bed
and imagining myself little
and Natalia big.

Translated by Iarina Albu

sleep, food

I was once the luckiest girl in the world.

I had grandparents, who lived in a village by a meadow,
a beach and an old forest,
all belonging to me and the other kids.

I had young and beautiful parents,
who lived their own lives,
at an ok distance from me.

Good friends, whom I shared everything with
and who hadn't yet left Romania.

I lived in a small, familiar town
in which I had a good time,
and I was glad I would soon be leaving it
for a bigger town.

I was once the most beautiful
the brightest, the most refined
the most in love
the one that had the least regrets
the most capable.

Days back then
seemed like comic book strips
with tangled, hard-to-read lines
but they were full of desire.

Now I'm nearing 40 and I'm living an appropriate life,
but, as far as desire goes,
I realize that there are more and more days
when all I want is

undisturbed slumber, in a vast space,
quiet and refreshing.

There are days at the end of winter
and then at the beginning of spring
when I can no longer keep up with my sleep,
with food,
and it seems as though I will never
return to a normal rhythm
with normal, ordinary days
with sleep, food.

Translated by Iarina Albu

test

Because, for a while now
the house I grew up in has been empty
every visit, for a few years now
it ends up being
a visit in nature.

Right now I'm at the edge of a forest.

I light a fire to keep warm
even though it's not yet night and it's not that cold.

I look for sticks under the crust of leaves
and imagine an installation.

This whole time I keep my headphones on,
so that the forest stays where it is,
like a static image on a screen
like a painted wall
because if I took them off
it would gain depth, dimension,
and the song of the birds or their encrypted cries,
the buzzing of the insects
would melt together and harm me.

I'm not glad to see the dark silhouettes of the children who,
after playing all afternoon on the riverside,
are being cast away by darkness
and are hurriedly walking home, further away from me.

I try to overcome a threshold
one at random
and stay here overnight.

Here, in nature.

The test is absurd and,
despite the courage I have now,
set up for failure.
Like any test.

Translated by Iarina Albu

tourism

A hotel with black windows
between two red hills
statues draped in velvet, burnt from place to place
embellished with pigeon feathers
plastic goddesses melted together
a dark and indiscernible mass
urban elements
sculpted balconies and mosaics
everything that is black
surrounded by a white haze
an obsolete, occult imaginary
this is how I interpret things
when I'm a tourist.

No post-industrial dynamic, nothing futuristic
because everything has already been surpassed and compromised
at most darkpop
and careful with the heart.

I feel waves of sadness that drown me
in the most ordinary moments
like when a car starts
or when the road is too long ahead
we are stuck in traffic
and blurry images seep through the window
with similar landscapes
when I'm a tourist.

I dream of a clear afternoon, no shadows
with a perfect cut-out of the sun
that stays inside the lines
or a singular moment of profound understanding
that contradicts the blueprint of a simple life

that I have no hopes of escaping
when I'm a tourist:
conventional tourism – oversized city –
internalized theatre.

Translated by Iarina Albu

rockballad

For some time now,
I've begun mystifying life more and more.

In the black car that climbs the hill to the church
on an ordinary day
I see the terminal stage, the poles of hope and capitulation
the torn soul, chewed up by doubt
the sharp conscience and the loosened tie
the dirty white collar of the shirt.

An atavistic desire
a head squashed like a snail
hidden in the leaves
and a classic scenario:
fugitive thoughts,
expeditious gestures,
misunderstanding.

A woman sitting beside it:
a cheek dirtied with mascara
a slightly loosened bun
disheveled strands of hair over her face.

The classic scenario:
addiction and unrequited love
will and worry over money.

In the rearview mirror,
a ceremony that ended badly:
a mess of tables and strange paintings made of sauces
glass shards and crumbs
music sloppily covered by conversation.

A barefoot woman that treads on slowly
through the disaster.

The pale sun over the hotel
the last people out smoking on the balcony,
men with stylish hair
and women in dresses.

Big, beautiful, well-fed dogs
running alongside the car
a patch of too-frail trees
that can't brighten up the place.

Strong metal arms inside
illuminated spectrally.

A vase on the table
in which a slim hand
adorned with a golden bracelet
threw some dirty flowers
rescued from the mud.

Later, the same woman,
her reflection in all the cars' windows
that start moving at the green light
the scarf with natural motifs escaped from her neck
blowing in the wind
caressing other people.

I see myself again in the basement of the cultural center
standing still among cassettes, with an empty glass in front of me
on which there are still fine traces of bloody mary,
personal history riddled with symbols,
the temporary fixes, the unsuitable finishing touches.

I see what happens on the world's stages on the screen
and it seems that nothing is about what it actually is
it's about something else, something personal, that I've forgotten.

I see the sun burning brightly over the meadow,
consuming the black smoke of the trucks burdened by grains,
on the way home
and the pale sun, from the summer kitchen's window,
back when no one had died yet
and everyone still worked
despite the dark and praising the light
in our garden.

Translated by Iarina Albu

a little song

I got a lot of good advice
that I didn't know what to do with
and look where I ended up
in solitude,
in seclusion,
not even with a grain of wisdom
my friend tells me while laughing
she forgot to show me
the old family photos
and for a while has just been touching them
in the pile in her lap
and looking at them by herself.

She had just found them again
in the former medicine cabinet
fixed in a wall
in her grandparents' house
and brought them as relics in this house
that she bought herself not long ago.

They're black and white photos
with zig-zag borders
folded and matte.

She gathers them and puts them away
she stretches her legs
and slides down in her chair
but it's not a comfortable position and presently
she gets up again.

In a way, us humans
she tells me with a serious face
we're all legendary, don't you think?

In the neighbor's yard,
the grass fills up
with white foam.

I realize that the neighbors
are probably washing their car or a rug
but I like to imagine
that people are even
thoroughly cleaning their gardens in this new neighborhood
at the edge of Bucharest
where the tension doesn't seem
to ever rise too high.

Humans of the future
with ten heads on one body
full of confidence, flexible and fast,
humans that make and break destinies
maybe even in parallel universes
like in Westworld.

Humans whose children play in brand-new gardens,
shiny,
where their voices resound clear at sundown,
scary, desperate and broken,
like between our communist blocks.

Translated by Iarina Albu

Radu Vancu

My heart was my personal utopia.

To be precise, my personal utopia was that my heart
no longer be an occasional, portable fridge, preserving
bottles of vodka and amputated limbs and precious
ice-cubes with fruit frozen inside them and piles
of eyeballs stacked like hay over dirt-mounds.

That my heart no longer be an occasional, portable
crematorium, in which my 6-year-old heart and my
10-year-old heart and my heart of 42 years, which is
when I will die, and my 60-year-old heart, and my
heart of 102 years, all burn together, snickering
like criminals who've gathered at a *pajama party*.

That my heart no longer serve (the most agonizing shit
& the most hideous) as a tiny, portable paradise like the little
heart of Christ in grandmother's neoprotestant bible from
Cisnadie, so pink and dazzling that it made me weep
from beauty and terror, to the point where I cut it out
with the small scissor of the pocketknife & buried
the paper heart under the mulberry, near the paradise of mice.

That my heart no longer be the paper toy you slice
when the urge arises, weeping from beauty and terror,
to bury it among your mulberries, in the paradise of your
sacrificial mice, knowing you will never have the courage

to cut with your pocketknife heart, Taborite[7] & rosy.

However desperately you crave this.

Translated by Alina Ştefănescu

---

[7] Taborite refers to a member of the radical wing of the Bohemian Hussites who rejected everything without direct biblical warrant except war (as waged fiercely under Ziska).

My utopia was your heart was paradise.
And I wrote it. As much as was possible.

Loneliness, coffee, quietude, pain. I can't enter
my own skull anymore.

Days pass through me like bullets from a death squad
through a corpse.

Any man is a dead-end—and writing the supreme abuse–
but from here, from where I am, it is truly impossible to write.

This is the text—this is the paradise—this is its entire power:

the dead of the future write the dead of the present

& the dead of the future write the dead of the past

& and this was the whole story from the beginning

& thus will it remain.

I've never done anything except footnote the dead;

drenched in light and pus, in ailing blood and hope,
a page is the splendor's open abscess.

Translated by Alina Ştefănescu

To write or not to write? Two halves of a question —
each one, a whole suicide.

In truth, all my literature should be read as failed
philosophy — practiced under covers.

I am a knife using a loud voice while cutting
itself —

making poems from the blood who gushes
from its metal blade.

Translated by Alina Ştefănescu

Buona notte, maestro who makes the child's eyes sparkle
as he carves a slice of Peruzzi pizza &
looks with love on the plastic BB-8[8]

purchased for 38 Euros at Disneyworld.
You are, as I tell you, a fantastic craftsman:
a constant smoothness is nothing in the face of

his eyes, devastated by happiness, the face of
his laughter passing through my flesh like light through the void.
I am tired, very tired, but I don't want to forget

to thank You for this.
(For the void of my flesh and the way his eyes illuminate
it. I hope You understand. I know You can grasp everything.)

I took his hand and rambled through Florence, rainy and empty
like me. Together we roamed the museums full
of beauty and voidness like me. And, suddenly,

at the Ufizzi, those eyes: the ones in Giotto's
baby Jesus. A child, practically still suckling,
with his eyes of devastating sadness.

I stood before him, found it hard to believe
the world continues spinning after those eyes.
But it keeps spinning, anyway.

How insensitive one must be to continue existing
after someone looks upon you with those eyes.
And after he no longer sees you.

---

[8] BB-8 (or Beebee-Ate) is a droid character in the Star Wars franchise, first appearing in the *Star Wars: The Force Awakens* (2015). A skittish but loyal astromech, BB-8 accompanied Poe Dameron on many missions for the Resistance, helping keep his X-wing in working order.

Surely even You are terribly exhausted,
after creating a man who drew a child
who wore those eyes on his face.

This must be devastating.
I'd be devastated in your place,
but You have the superpower of resisting

the eyes of small children. My sole superpower
is to hold the child's hand and enter the Disney store
& find joy in the illumination

of his tiny flesh & gaze. At this point, I confess,
I'm glad the whole thing keeps spinning.
It's late, I'm extremely exhausted;

in me, You failed to regulate the constants,
sometimes my own flesh illuminates,
now it is simply something aged and sad.

The way rain falls rapidly, then slows to a trickle.
He caresses the plastic BB-8,
and lifts those luminous eyes towards me—

my plastic heart is a BB-8 with all the
batteries drained. I don't want to forget
to thank You for this.

You created a world of miserable people
that write psalms for You about beauty.
About the toys of children. About illuminated eyes

and devastators drawing us back in splendor.
Maestro, the sad humans tip their hats
& thank You. For this sky—and limitless sadness.

Still a constant elegance, this.
Sadness is our superpower
and its will, forever, being completing.

Translated by Alina Ștefănescu

If humans were actually living, they'd need to scream without
ceasing several times a day.

If books were actually living, these pages would need to
        scream without ending.

Translated by Alina Ștefănescu

Dan Sociu

i'm so soured on the internet and books
it rains between buildings, the wind makes waves on puddles,
i want nothing external, nothing deep
only to eat and watch comedy
pity i can't chew the teeth from my face
since humans are so stupid in their lives

i busted my own a long time ago at a rock show
and don't believe i like rock anymore
                 or almost at all
but i believe i like almost anything with rice
there was a time when i wanted to vomit
                 whenever i saw it

nor do i wash the dishes, i'll wash them in the morning
mankind also wants commercial breaks from life

Translated by Alina Ştefănescu

we are only moments or
moments, it is adolescence
who passes by on majestic skates
and forms figure-of-eights and undulates, slowly

or still her who passes
this way, without skates and steps
the same, she even rushes a little and
she leaves me cold

Translated by Alina Ștefănescu

but i wasn't really
on an abandoned street
the full-bodied Roma in house dresses on the sidewalk
having a smoke
with their elders of the white hair
and yellowed beard
who rested their feasts
after a midnight grilling session

teen girls with dark skin, in white blouses
with belly buttons and nerve
                    in their voices,
raising their legs up,
they danced with illuminated phones
i kept hearing them
and sometimes i could also glimpse
when the night patrols tore them
from obscurity

best to tell you instead how i always made
the mere surface of the infernos
because this, too, is my hell, my fall—
corrupting the surface
i was more stuck on the present than those girls
lit by lanterns
day belonged to the day, night to night
and morning only to morning

i lived in the now, for the now, glued without rest
to that which can be seen and be felt
and i know so well only those who have lived this way
can understand and believe me
the rest of you, i remember vaguely, wasted yourselves in
the darkening classroom

well-behaved and well-dressed, straight and orderly and
terrified, with nails bitten to nubs

at the blood of my fear at tomorrow's uncertainty, of the day after
tomorrow, of the day after that, of fear
life disappears in drip drip your life, i saw
how the psychoparasites rotted you
how their shadows possessed you, how you let yourselves
be ruined, with dog-like submission
slaves to their envy, hypnotized by the promises
of the day after the day after tomorrow

they turned girls into stars with their lanterns
in short dreams, in a flash
three months of summer scorched the air and
the asphalt like in Marrakesh
the girls' skin burned more brightly than gold on rings,
their youth inflamed,
long years had passed since i, too, had perished
and surpassed sadness

life outside life, when one tries to touch
the walls and feels oneself touching
but they are so unreal that you could leave yourself on them
and push them
as if they were nothing, like the mime in a pantomime,
when there is nothing concrete to push,
like a berserker on the empty battlefield when
nothing remains to murder

i was still agitating between realities
though actually emptied by reality
i won't try to say what cannot be spoken,
whether in joy or in pathos,
the dead man who walks between lives has nothing

but the living shared in words
and what he'd say to the alive would make their vineyards
endless voids in the mind

i left the places i didn't like and
places i liked i stayed in
having only immediate purposes, alive for an instant, to
find on the floor another cigarette butt
to move myself two steps closer to the sun,
to trample the town after smiling girls
to find my bed for the night or let
the whole night go by on foot

i ate only vodka and beer and
sometimes a hot dog with pleasure
i didn't have money and my ass ached, what i lacked
i could have stolen
but i wanted nothing, to walk, to loaf, to
read, a handful of comrades and the same day again
and again, when there was no sun, there was the heat from bars,
laughter and sleep anywhere with boots on my feet

and then Ştefan the photographer took me into his home
without electricity and water, with cold walls
i dwelled for three years there the childhood winters
of socialism in the 1980's
when every member of the family slept in the same room
in a pile and still a pile
there was Stefan, the girls Didi and Anto and Cici, Bogdan,
Gabi, Daniel and Dorin and the gigantic cat named Rada

Translated by Alina Ştefănescu

i was born to be cavalier, a poet warrior
perfected lover defender of saints
he who bewitches and soothes and stirs up
and resurrects them to life through words
a man who makes them feel great in his presence and
forget the tiny terrors
supreme realist, who looks cool with
legs over an abyss at the peak of whatever mountain

because he knows the abyss can be a thousand
kilometers deep, it doesn't matter
it only matters that the rock is solid, that the wind
beats gently and the mind is woken
and because i knew that life held me, i drank
at Deva, on the ruins
with my legs over the abyss, the same in Iasi in Târgușor
on campus, in the dorms

seeing that life wanted me,
i descended on the highway atop my skateboard
rode kilometers in the rain, at night, between
cars, but life did not want her boy to fall,
smart and handsome, courageous brat and
when everything slipped
on the wet plank and the wheels trembled on asphalt
even then she still wanted him right there,
again and again, between the headlights,
          with her burning hips, the same
every time I had a mission, and now
my mission was to bring grandmother ice cream
two wafers in a plastic bag,
                    in a crazed race
to get to the village
                    before they began melting
and they were the best of my bubbles with

people, a complete bubble, like all bubbles i entered
since there were always many others, permanent bubbles and
momentary clusters, almost the same i loved them
how i loved almost everything the same, every day
there were days and any moment was a complete bubble
i approached my life with snout extended, but only studied
the life of the living and that's why i didn't go to school

since around the age of 12, when i was left fatherless, and
i liberated myself, in happiness and pathos
from his severe stewardship, from another six years of
school, i was present for ten months gathered
when i was there, my gaze nailed beneath the desk,
buried in some book with adventures and nothing
it said or tried to tell me
altered my heart's nobility even slightly

and i was still too little, since junior high, through
about tenth grade, i liberated myself from all
and came to school only for amusement and
to score another ten on my report card, to show them i could
i never learned anything, i only went
directly into the world's foundations and returned
in the same instant with a resolution, my past
schools can attest, this is how i was and was made
now i know i am as weak as a wind blade
inconsistent as a word
because i know i am concrete, from flesh
and time and i can be broken
in two now by death

the way a phone rings suddenly

because i almost died in actuality and my family
is almost entirely dead

and my diabetic grandmother, to whom i snuck
    ice cream

died, impoverished, and before dying she asked me
if i had eaten

and my dad died too
and he squeezed my little hand near the ambulance
and my grandfather also died with his disposition
grinning
and uncle Ion also died, oh how much i loved him too
and i love him still
i keep wanting to weep since they are no longer living
and nothing more comes to me
nothing comes to me
gone, too, are the days filled with truths
living in the world, living and feeling
when we fought
and when we laughed and made jokes
and they loved me and i loved them and was luminous
for them, because there was someone to see me
sleeping through summer, all of us in the orchard
on blankets of grass, under quilts, under branches
in open air
and the dogs went off in the village or it sounded like
a wail
and my anxious grandmother worried aloud
and my sleepy grandfather grumpily reassured her
and our heads drowned in pillows, weighted
beneath the dark-spaces between stars
only our breaths remained audible
and the crickets and frogs and then not even them
only the silence of dreams, mysterious
and in bones, the animal warmth of home

Translated by Alina Ştefănescu

Medeea Iancu

BLESS YOUR HEART, history,

bless your dress, you
who said no,

Bless the history of rape
and rape's mother,

Bless you, history!

And what do you know about your country?
You know nothing,
Nothing and let me explain:
You know nothing!

And I write another poem about
Rape, a poem blessed by god about
Rape, and I write another poem about
Violence, bless you, violence

And I don't believe in countries, bless
You no-country,
And I cannot sleep and
I cannot eat,
Bless no body and
You, injustices,

Blessed you, fury, blessed
Repetition, bless you, humiliation and
Bludgeons who beat me in the schoolyard be

blessed and the director who
Said:
You shouldn't complain, it's a nothing
All of it, you should be capable of
defending yourself, I

Can't do anything,
You are at
Fault.

And the policeman who raped
The woman, bless him, and
The romanian police who did
Nothing, bless them

And the romanian police who blamed
the victim, bless them,

Bless you, history:

Where a language was lost,
a body was
humiliated.

Every mother who
leaves her country
In order

To work in
Another,

Leaves a
Kid without
language.

Every mother
Here

Weeps in
Romanian.

Translated by Alina Ștefănescu

MY LANGUAGE has become a

War.

I am afraid,
You are afraid,
They are afraid,

I
Was history, not
Biography.

Power lives in our museums and we
Praise it.

I
Is political, so I was born in
Fear and
Death,

Help me create pride, not
     Shame.

No body is
Booty:
Help me create pride, not

Shame.

Translated by Alina Ştefănescu

MY TEARS fall in

Foreign languages.

All milk is violent within.
My inside is violent it grew like

Dead bodies. I chew
God and

Bleed. I beg all dead things, I
Beg

Blood, itself. The violence inside me is a
Bombed house. I breathe

And another child
Dies. I wipe my

Tears as my hand closes the eye of another
Child. I walk and my stride makes

Tombs. I stay quiet but my silence
Kills them.

I beg all dead things, I
Beg

Blood. I seek a word across days and I find
Cadavers.

The violence crumbles inside me like a scorched
House. The violence inside me is a

Leviathan. I chew god and discover

Cadavers.

Translated by Alina Ştefănescu

I am not

Enough for
This century, all
Italics, I

Am excess, the splendor of a
Beast, I
Am superb with
Blood on my haunches.

I am Jack Gilbert and June Jordan and
Adrienne Rich when she
Wrote:

The will to change begins in the body not
In the mind, my

Politics is in my body, accruing and expanding
With every act of

Resistance and
Each of my failures
Locked in the closet at 4 years old I beat the wall
With my body

That act is
In me
Still

I
Am not
A market
For fish.

My lungs preserve
BBC headlines,

My language, 1 Tb of
Violence.

I am Kevin Young and Amiri Baraka
and Rita Dove and Paul Celan,

I am Frederick Seidel and Lucille Clifton,
I am H. L. Hix and

We are
An Army

I
Form verses like the shots of
Serena
Williams,

All italics like
Flags and

Flames,
Like

Embryos.

I am the
Party,

Disco ball
Spinning:

Language is

who you serve

Or
What you have

Inherited?

I am not a
Market for

Fish, I
Am

The threat

Translated by Alina Ştefănescu

Răzvan Țupa

urban

a surreal locomotive's cab in the middle of the city
an abandoned house
that we climb and where we throw electrodes at each other then we can
wear some red t-shirts sweat pants
i am on drumul taberei and i'm thinking of buying something light and refreshing
for cătălin and oana anyway the ones i visited were always
somewhere else i will tell them about marius and his rage riding the old people
at some point a shadow of the coffee cup will open building
on my rolled-up sleeve a visual kiosk that could be all
a gigant body will grow from my head and unfold upon the city
you don't have to believe me you'll see then it will rain like it hasn't rained before

Translated by Iarina Albu

liquidities

After everyone had left, I went down to the warehouse. To get to the basement
you would go down from the second floor through under the Cantacuzino palace on
    some narrow
stairs through pitch black darkness to the first switch on the ground floor and then
under to a button in the underground hallway.
Everything happened in the dark until there. The walls made of
rough concrete were waiting for anything I could
imagine and the great bank of memories
started doing its job. What you re-
member, what you can imagine, pick a face, pick a
name and everything else falls into place the way you tell it to. And then I didn't un-
    derstand
anything other than that if you move faster the
great frights can no longer reach you
with their minuscule can-openers wedged under
my eyelids. I pressed lightly and around the button that was hanging by
only two threads from the low ceiling. Doors. All locked. All with their
own pattern, just like you.

Translated by Iarina Albu

the way you are

I can be silent because I can say anything

what your gestures signify
what they know of the warm touch in answer to a question
that no one is there to ask
where you stand on things that not even you are sure of
I'm talking deterministic uncertainties
of the rural science of silence where you fail to mention
the field at the back of the house the spacious quiet all around
breathing all on its own

Translated by Marina Sofia

totem 3

to wake in the sallow gloom at night
with a light sequence imprinted on my retina white flames hemming my eyes
looking at the warm soles of your feet
caught in the twist between dust and air
layered sunlight
announces noon the hours press upon us with belaboured breath
the lines someone drew in the grass around us
with lined pages from a torn notebook by the fence

music at last in harmony with silence

to search for my watch on the night table to not switch on the light
to mistake all these perfectly distinct impressions with your movements
about which I cannot say much

other than that they rustle and linger

Translated by Marina Sofia

by the light of urban birds

in the evening yes you leave beneath the orange neons of the shopwindows
the objects displayed among the clouds parading in front of you
not slaking your thirst in the slightest
we were promised complete hyrdration a fluid kind of love that could go right to the
    rough edge
of your eyelids from morning to night dreaming of leaving
without having to say was that all

Translated by Marina Sofia

traces on the ankle

in that short half-hour when everyone you see
overwhelms you with their beauty and keeps up appearances
i beg you do not undress do not undress yet

no discernible music can be heard only frail signals
for this time the air does not cling to you
or beg you with your own hands your fingers clenched

in invisible cracks that might not even exist in the real world

the little chinese cars with their comforting roar protecting that distant region
inhabited by the single person you don't know
the single person you are not and that no toy soldier can isolate

the invisible cracks that only hold the crush

you try to escape from as fast as your legs will take you and when they won't you
    crawl
in the hope of reaching the other side of the world somehow

Translated by Marina Sofia

PAIN IS A FOREIGN LANGUAGE A Romanian body knows better than to
choose that *for then there would be no more excuses for the easy pains* **for this one
you need to stay here with your entire body** *you could be an ornament a sticker*
and one of these days the rhythm of your breathing will disappear *all by itself*
or the reverse **my hands ready to receive the calm** *like a sandwich* I waited in
the coach station **until I was in tears** the air tasted of fresh fruit *I had prepared eve-
rything; everyone was there* all I had to do was watch the busy-bustle evening
crowds *decide which part of me to consume first* they could not believe I could
stand up serenely **minding my own business** *in my mother tongue like a skate-
board*

Translated by Marina Sofia

V. Leac

at my place

i bring wrappers upstairs
the room is full of post-it notes
in the living room a mess of consonants in slippers
the bathroom – ventilation holes
not a lot can be said about us

the salmon skeleton in the trash could have a good
career
but what skeleton has a career you ask yourself
we know of a few that did
your long dresses are just as mysterious
as the magazine named fishing adventures
the hallway in the apartment hides a murderer
what a weird relationship what faith ties us together
maybe the breasts in the chinese cup

the skeleton goes downstairs now it's in the trash
it's morning the balcony door slams
of course it's not about me
it's the old story with the fan

the chocolate bar wrappers have an ecological effect
they're in the garden behind the garage
now the decor of the apartment has changed
two insipid clones speak of long-gone days
about the disappearance of the possibility of an island.

Translated by Iarina Albu

no strings attached

i looked at my hands with guilt
now i realize that everything was a mess
M. was installing XP on your computer and i kept repeating it's impossible
after a bottle of wine blood tests blood tests blood tests
what effect do cakes and cigarettes have
on teachers that work their asses off
you told me you would be fair to me
that we'd split everything equally
I was always fascinated by couples who
discussed love in technical terms

now i'm in a park in front of the wagon factory
and behind me in a gooseberry tree
are three children talking about backpacks
i started making phone calls desperately
to somehow get closer to reality
in the end I left the children there in the goosberry tree
on the way i improvised a song:

when all the petrol will be gone
you will come back to me
when all the gas will be gone
you'll be mine again
when all the petrol will be gone
the luxury automobiles will turn in their keys
and the world will be a little less sad
when all the factories close

Translated by Iarina Albu

b a d o r w o r s e

In the train old men represent curiosity they die
with you around their necks where you from what medicine pension
remarks about the weather the world today
etc etc etc

Oh, it's good to have ice skates
It's good to slide all on your own

beside old men, not with indifference
and pity, but with an intelligent disposition
that knows how to give naïve and banal answers
hot cocoa and the window seat.

It sucks to be stuck in bed blocked by fat,
to hate and despair that the car is broken.
Curious like a mobster's child that wants the seat by the window.
Connections are optional,
not everyone makes it here.

It's a simple mirage fueled by imaginary catastrophes.
It's the unbearableness that creates violent sentiments
and atrocities in the domestic space.
Feelings that make you stay hidden and rub your face with your palms.

You may think I suffer from oscillating dementia,
but you can't possibly think I'm indifferent and tolerant.
Personal notes, small introspections in the land of hypocrisy.
You kick a wrapper with your foot: an indifferent way
of punishing envy.

Oh, what spleeeeeendor
to see this much pollution

You haven't punished anyone, you mostly stay inside
and smoke, you don't push away the dog with your foot.
You let yourself be led by a sleepy conscience in
the zone named monoideal: a place where you transferred
your hopes and pleasures.

I reconstruct myself
in all the heroes I hate and I invent a political
doctrine in which individuals know only pain and panic.
A reservation of domestic-hostile feelings.

Translated by Iarina Albu

SOLIDEAL

The terrace for confusion is to be preferred
There's a few of us that know we're never going to leave the perimeter
It's like meeting 1 pathological liar that
You can't get rid of

When I met Erika
In combination with halls they say it wreaks
It's so pleasant and terrifying to touch matter
Some say that we have to return to values
Everyone considered good
Defends themselves and transports their things further

Geneticists say you can see
Someone's wickedness in the shape of their nails
These sensitive and introverted guys that don't see a way out
Their soul is a rough terrain haunted by specters
And suspicion
They know before going to the doctor's office what problems you have
They are no different from those that walk with their living strollers
Through the park and wake up from their reveries
When some people they know
Bend over the stroller and make noises
What a tiring profession politeness is

Whoever smiles at you demonstrates
That fiction is possible
Size matters It makes new types of sentiments appear
Quit the bullshit and think of something more sophisticated

If you're a revolutionary don't take your briefs off
There was a movie with monks lost in the desert
Some masked people sold jam and opium
What won't you do for the effect?

Who smiles at you mistakes you
You pull the rope and the parachute opens
The parachute protects you from gravity

"Do you like omelets?" you asked
"Yes, and documentaries."
An aggressive hand grabs something out of a drawer.
A belligerent hand leads you through reality.
After a while everyone ceases to be ok.

Translated by Iarina Albu

Tiberiu Neacşu

The Elevator Poem

And after I called them by their names and you assured me they don't exist
you brought me to their house and let them smell my hands.

And I was very surprised to find that you had no
Hands, no name, just

Nails, tables, a coffer with FRAGILE written on it –
surely someone keeps the past in there.

And I sobbed like a child, with snot and hiccups
and my tiny shoulders shuddered just so.

Candy, toys were to them
the offspring of a hiccupping child.

I let them, I admitted nothing.

Then I called them by their names and you assured me
you won't let them smell my hands.

Translated by the poet with Iarina Albu

Of the Middle Ages

That day I don't remember who
saved whom. We saved each
other, phrases about medieval kings
babbled in our heads,
the slutty maids were undoing
their corsets after the appetizer, the dying
clowns at a sign of the opposable thumb,
the candles that stank of lanolin,
the hustle, the bustle of the servants. The first
time, I reassembled the pieces of the clay vase
and smoothed its jagged edges –
the hands slid as they did in childhood
when we would draw hopscotch on the cobblestone
pavement: on cracks we stopped
the line; the chalk became dirty with soil
and it was hard to make it draw again
on the next stone; we guessed the line through the gaps;
we knew what could and couldn't be skipped. We would throw
the rod from the ground up and
back with precision – the mending
was smooth. Then we would erase our
tracks and push away
the big pile of glass shards.
Until we found another amidst the laughs
and the smacks that no longer mattered.
The next day, through the big bones cleaned
by royal cats we rearranged
the dishware exactly as it was.
We needed sleep. We went to bed
there, among the mutton legs
that seeped juice through the floorboards.
The animals licked the musty fat

and wandered, one by one, next to the royal bed
to get petted.

That was when I finally heard
the megalomaniac city with all
its sick organs beautifully arranged.

Translated by the poet with Iarina Albu

The Gift

of My Brother

I'm writing to you from the entrails of a blue whale. Small
green pastures grab the light and turn the ocean
upside down. Wild horses run through the grass
and throw dandelion dust over the pasture with their hooves.
Further down, on the path, children play ball, parents
clink their glasses with desperation.

The frogs climb lotus leaves and croak
the same words generation after generation. Pay
attention to the mosquitoes – they suffocate your skin and devour

your red blood cells with relish. Dragonflies, transparent
and lucid, dream of being someone other than
dragonflies. A lily rises from under the black incandescent

earth. Here and there, on the fresh grass,
ticks and ladybugs grab the soil and smash the sun
into a thousand pieces. Snails hide with darkness

under their eyelids. Worms gather circles of maroon
bodies, the lizards freeze, warm up, they
lose their tails and equilibrium at the same time.

I bring you this plankton to keep in your palms –
a globe and so many wasted years.

Translated by the poet with Iarina Albu

Looking at dad

To see my father not seeing me with
one eye, and with the other
fogged by glaucoma—iced connections
in his head, scrambled heaps of images,
the seaside, the earthquake—I remember
sitting at the same table. Smoking the same
cigarette, drinking beer. "Tell me,"
he said, "do you have any brain in that
head of yours? Do I have to shake it out
for you to understand?" I shrugged.
Then a short slap, and here I was,
red left cheek, not knowing, not
seeing where it came from. And then again.
When it all ended, he came to hug me
as if someone else had done it. Like I'd
forgotten everything and was ready to feel
the smoke entering my lungs again—a friend
told me it's strange that I still write
about smoking—, still, with no difficulty
I clean my face and smile and love him.
And now, when I look at him looking through me
I catch a bright reflection of the light
right under the blue, matte eye, right
when it gets cloudy and wet, and he remembers.

Translated by the poet with Iarina Albu

For you I

For you I jump over
puddles when it rains
and get my Clarks
all muddy and wet.
In this new neighborhood
I live, and in you
I live like a deranged
egg in a sick bird. Not
flying, necrophagous,
little brother of poverty
and starvation.
You are my most attentive
foe, you grisly friend.
I only know you,
really, and so I hesitate
to leave
I surf you,
familiarly. I sniff
the dusty air and find
pleasure in my allergies.
I stumble against
bureaucracy, yet
find it comfortable.
For you I've kept
people in, minimize my
chances, possibly wrecked
lives, who knows. Yet
I think of you
and never let
you down. I speak
another language
than yours, I claim
you're horrible,

I rant at you in my own
brain dry as prunes—out of
which Grammy used
to make stew
when fasting. Its
sweet taste would spring
over our mouths,
its incense would
purse our insides
to stop hunger. The bread
would be too hard,
yet dipped in it,
would be delicious
—I spare you my views,
and I don't go out.
For you I've shouted
On the streets
to show I care.
I pay my taxes, buy
things, have debts, credit
cards, mortgage, subscriptions
—phone, internet,
cable, electricity, gas—
do not budge when everybody
tells me to move on.
I chip on my words,
never knowing anything,
really. Sober and centered,
I'm satisfied and refuse
everything. And still
you're not moving.
Someday you'll see
me leaving. You're
pushing me out,

Romania, outside, where I don't
know anything. Where birds
and eggs are the same.
And die the same.

Translated by the poet with Iarina Albu

The Room

I opened my eyes and the air was hard
to breathe. The morning was hot,
the sky was clearing up in the south,
the leaves were rustling, tamed by the sun.

It was unconceivable for the soles of your feet to be burnt,
it was unconceivable to not be you anymore
and speak the same way anymore:

My brain is no one,
it follows no one and doesn't know
what's what.

Only the body breathes,
only the body lives here
where I don't know where I am.

Translated by the poet with Iarina Albu

Rita Chirian

you are younger than me

you turn happy when winter comes

when it snows
I remember
a glass square
poplars like skirts
the night when
my feet stayed
frozen until
morning

but you are younger than me

i can't envy you

Translated by Iarina Albu

& we drove a thousand kilometers

in less than twenty-four hours

in a village in moldova
an old lady sat begging on the side of the road
watching the cars that passed her on their way to the mountains

we passed her fast

we continued on for over a kilometer
until we decided to go back

if the fog doesn't lift
we won't get home by nightfall

Translated by Iarina Albu

shaky photograph

and if the heart of the hummingbird beats 1000
times per minute doesn't it say to itself i'm tired? –
my heart beats so so fast? –
the equilibrium bird inside the wing tornado.

the elephants return each year to the place a calf died.

i don't remember how the shadow
fell, i don't know
the license plate number of the car
that honked long after that.
i'm the animal encouraged to live –

you say, the coldness of the bird is clinical &
look how much color in the loss of adherence –
here, in the fixed world – me, to me, mine –
& how big your heart is in death –
(new informal conversations)
i look at the passing cars – and how beautifully
the waters of death rise
in the hippocampus – and how many
representations
of being
alone

Translated by Iarina Albu

abendphantasie

their beauty resembles the oriental cuisine
small & clean animals, with sweet marrow –
water babbling a lullaby.

how the metal reflects the cut through the bone.
how the blade.

the chef says, tell me your nightmare,

the chef says, i found it and it didn't make sense,

the chef says, in the morning
a wrinkled, absurd place, something to satisfy & hurt harder.

peace comes late
(insects in which we see each other,
almost crushing each other)

beauty is our humble desperation

Translated by Iarina Albu

kitsch & porn

be good and clean, take out the sack filled to the brim with treats, push strollers for
    butterflies, don't say, ingeborg, your eyes are so green this fall, learn to tell left
    apart from right quickly, to steer carriages over objects – when everything is beau-
    tiful & bitter, and everyone is lenient – see the strange but painless shape un-
    screwing, say, there is no big and small, let's not adopt stupid habits, say, I'm
    from a bad seed, the air is musty all around but you're an experienced diver, the
    kitsch & porn heart out of which all you want are flies and stitches, love like a
    parasite-ridden belly – in the morning when you lie about blood, about the stitch
    in between your legs and then again, in the tank riddled with algae, roaring as
    you'd hear in a shell.

Translated by Iarina Albu

what is there left to hate

the striptease stopped at the right time

now we won't let any light
seep in.

we devoured
the synthesizing exercises,
the manic episodes,
the strange womanly compulsions
that organize
their nest
flawlessly.

in the end
the empty glass
which I smacked
against my teeth
from time to time.

Translated by Iarina Albu

Elena Vlădăreanu

All of a sudden, everyone started talking about money. No one was talking about money back in 2008, during the financial crisis. Your manuscript was accepted, you said thanks, even if you had to change the sale percentage you got in the contract all by yourself, from 10% to 5%. Or in *no financial claims.* You said thanks and you said something else as well. Always: *I know, we're in a crisis, I understand.* And you would go home and wait for the crisis to end, accumulating symbolic capital.

A few years later we all found out that in fact the crisis wasn't ending, a new one was just beginning. From bad to worse. And then we started talking about money.

Some wrote love letters to money.

Others filled a museum with all sorts of trinkets, key chains with characters from cartoons, plastic tanks, books you could buy per meter, bound in "eco leather", toy money. Every object has a set price. You buy, your name is written in a notebook, you get the change in pennies, and the money goes in an aquarium where it will swim until the end of time.

I haven't always been 62 kilos. But even when I weighted 40, I still looked like I was 60.
Big hips, big boobs, big bones. Slouched shoulders, just like my mom's.
When I'd just met my now-husband and I was very much in love, he once took a picture of me while I was making him French fries. I look like a housewife, I told him, like an auntie. Delete it. What, aren't you? he said.
I was.
But artists aren't. And I hated that.

One day, a poet got undressed while reading his poems.
The gesture became viral.
For a few hours, his favorite word used on the internet was:
Shlong.
Shlong!
Let's spell it together: S-H-L-O-N-G!

alongside *naked poetry.*
A white, young, beautiful, heterosexual man. A pure-blood artist.
But what if:

They started financing their life, writing
applications applications applications applications applications applications

I also wrote
applications applications applications applications applications applications

Most likely
I'm not a good application writer

I don't know how to sell myself

X and Z and Y got the residency
X, Y, and Z are good application writers.

Five years from now, in an interview, X, Y, and Z: *A and B recommended us for the*
   residency, they are wonderful writers – and humans! – that we're also friends with.
   That's how we got in.

A woman, not that young, fat, saggy boobs, cellulite
two children by her side
Etc.
Etc.
practicing *naked poetry?*
Really?!

I like colorful clothes, artists dress in black. *All black.* I don't smoke, artists smoke. I
   don't do drugs, I don't drink. Artists… whatever.

I told myself I'll lose weight. I cut out sweets, fats, I started swimming,
running in the park.

What if I also tried rhinoplasty?

Bought an orthosis, straight back, straight shoulders.

A radical wardrobe change.
I am a raven.

Breast reduction surgery.
Artists are androgynous, REPRODUCTION is written all over me
Save the species.
Housewife.
Mother.
Short, big hips, thighs, fat rolls, boobs, slouchy shoulders.

Artists don't reproduce.
Master Manole flies off the roof, his wife is buried alive inside the wall,
with no offspring.

What should an artist look like?
I pick a magazine. I opened it. Maybe this is what an artist should look like.
Handsome. Well-groomed beard. Impeccable haircut. Dark circles from work-
    ing. The buttoned-up shirt. You can tell it was expensive. Waistcoat. A hand
    in his waistcoat. Oh, a silver cuff. A slim body.
Photogenic. Beard. Did I already say that? I did.
He looks straight ahead. With confidence. And a tinge of playfulness.
Playfulness.
Playfulness.
Well, yes, playfulness.
A touch of magic.
Escapism.
Some gastronomy.
Elegance.
Because it's all about attitude.

Hello. I am the Romanian Cultural Institute.
Hello. I am the European Cultural Institute.
Hello. I am the Center for Artists' Residencies and Grants.
We all need you.
You're smart, you're our project.

You're our ray of sunshine in tomorrow's sky.

We believe in you.

We want to invest in you.

You better smarten up and tell us a few words about yourself.

Describe your activity.

Talk about your artistic statement.

What makes you stand out from all the other artists?

Demonstrate!

Justify!

Explain!

Argue!

Prove!

Answer:

Why do you want money from us?

Really now, would you actually be able to write that?

It's not alright, it's not okay at all.

Explain to us how your work relates to the residency or the grant
we're offering.

Something about the charm of the place. Maybe about the food. Culture.
Museums…

C'mon, c'mon, you're the creative one, we can't teach you how to do it.

Stop. I, the Romanian Cultural Institute, am not offering anything
right now, you didn't convince me.

Young people better waste their good years waiting,
to ripen up a bit.

Prove to us you're original.

But not too original, *more is less.*

But please, please don't tell us you're over 35!

I want to invest in you and brand you as an emerging artist.

A big EMERGING ARTIST written on your forehead.

How the hell can I do that if you're old?

So under 35, please!

Translated by Iarina Albu

Ruxandra Novac

23.

From the way you were educated. From brutality which isn't actually brutality. From
control. From attention. With the eyes squeezed, wide open, squeezed, wide
open. From meetings of cellophane, thrown on bodies. From the confusion after
— which sews the colours together — something to modify you, an inverse
prayer of the heart. From delicacy. From dissolution. From persistence. From
asymmetry. From temporal bruise. From neons. From attention — from barriers
— from a heigh. From fear. From terror. From brutality, which is of the brain.
From skin. From saliva, which comes from hidden places. From attention. From
attention. From attention. From attention.

Translated by Iarina Albu

31.

From a synth. Out of loneliness. Out of airports.

Out of crowne plaza on the 31st of december, out of the violet lights shaped like holiday wishes, i was there or rather someone was. Willow in the winter, diluted eyes.

When were you the closest to obtaining a little control? In 2008, in a hotel in brusells, there was a movie, i was smoking in my room, and beneath me there was an israeli party, i could see their frozen faces through the floor, it was his luxury and paleness from outer space and they had those fragile ages, 60-65, when everything is possible, but from another world, like a polar bear you can see through a slit, a liquid stuck at some point in the circuits. I was all alone, i paid attention to everything. Closing your eyes tightly, going back into the world for no reason other than being cold, intact, for the empty morning, strangled by the cold. I went back for her, we went to the botanique, 1st of january, education is done like this, glued to foreign bodies, to objects licking the skin, protruding its vulnerabilities, creating zones, and you know you can only do this with something truly foreign.

Translated by Iarina Albu

46.

Yellow waterlilies — the color of madness it is said. Sometimes there are these arcs which transport people into other ages, people very different from us would say it is a reparation, that they're being offered another chance. But you look so different sometimes and your gaze isn't yours anymore.

Unknown emotion, where it takes you. It is said that it is a particular language, but it is a network of pins. It is said that it is like a painting, and it really is, you carry it everywhere. Waves upon waves upon the heart, they turn you back from the path, the little crab has found its nourishment in a corner of the wall and torments you.

Translated by Iarina Albu

54.

Airplanes among stars. The sky down low, crashed among the lakes. Technicalities, survival. A constellation above us, the city destroyed, rounding around in your rhythm, you are not in the bayou, it is a shadow of yours caught between planets, a house abandoned beyond its margins, a lacerated body falling. The water divides you, it leaves you on the margins, a bit of clarity, a few fixed words, detached from music and chemical flickers, it's your small part, with the root almost burnt. You try to say them aloud, to have them hold you somehow. They are about kicking out or including, but they are spoken by children. The structure changes, now it moves slowly before you, you can touch it. Forest-field, then empty buildings in the fog, their deafening tick, big-forest,big-black-field, newfoundland.

Translated by Iarina Albu

Adrian Diniş

X- rays

I have no fancy photos, only
X-rays. Were I to line them up,
my X-rays and my test results,
I could very nearly make a body for myself,
disfigured, sure, but turned inside-out,
so all deformities would lie within. My disease
looks beautiful on an X-ray,
radiant. Patches of light
on a darkened form. I stare
for hours at those X-rays; my eyes know
those flecks of light harbor death,
need to be removed, sliced with a scalpel,
exterminated. And it has no meaning
at all – except maybe in poetry,
where, just like in my X-rays,
diseases can look beautiful and radiant
and somehow it all makes sense.

Translated by Marina Sofia

The Goldfish in the Whisky Glass

Who needs her anyway when I've got you,
Jack Daniel and Johnnie Walker?
Oh, Bloody Mary! A kiss stings like a measure of whisky,
but tears cleanse you a hundred times better.
Bloody Mary, how many men have died for you?

I called out until
someone answered in your name. It wasn't you!
Or maybe it was you. I was too drunk to notice.
The name should not matter,
we've been naming things since Adam and Eve.

All the poets in the city, all the drunks in the city,
all of us together looking for a word for love or a drink.
I'm proud of my predictions – made just a few hours ago.
I just called to say I love you...
because if I called you any later, I'd be drunk and you wouldn't believe me.

There's a fly drowning in my glass. If I knew how to swim,
I'd jump in to rescue it. I ask myself once more
if I could learn to swim like others have,
thrown in at the deep end. Like the poor chicks in a binbag, stealing my soul.

I don't want to drink anymore.
And, although no one needs to die to be remembered,
that dead fly going from shit to shit throughout its brief life
makes me feel less alone. Except I don't want anyone to die
simply so I can feel better about myself.

The goldfish in the whisky glass
wave at me and tell me it will be all right on the night.
Will it?

Translated by Marina Sofia

Classifieds

For sale: a soul. Possibly refurbished. You can pay by card. I'll even accept meal vouchers. Price: negotiable. No agencies. Serious offers only, please, from the Devil. Don't call in the early hours of the morning with a woman's voice telling me that you love me. Do not claim my granny has died and you miss me, and are waiting for me. That I should go to church every now and then and pray for her, may God bring us together soon, for you've made cabbage pie for me, just the way I like it. And that I should bring that girl who keeps phoning at night, that they would like to meet her, she must be a nice girl if she loves me and I love her. Don't call me from Vodafone, because I'm a valued customer and you'd like to offer me a better monthly plan, with free minutes of roaming abroad, perhaps in the netherworld, or try to stuff that prize tablet down my throat. Please don't call me from multinationals interviewing me for a job. Would the Devil please refrain from calling if there is nothing better on offer. I am open to offers from devils from other faiths.

Translated by Marina Sofia

Things that never touch me

Bad music and your love
Pictures of you at the seaside
Morning light through the shutters
Dawn in the pictures of you at the seaside
Nighttime sleep
You calling the elevator in the morning
The bus when I need it
The love of normal people
Holding hands on the street
Their love makes me sick

Translated by Marina Sofia

Candle on water

You forget the tap on in the bathtub
you forget you need to love back
and suddenly someone dies because you
forgot the gas hob on

My love for you has forgotten
the slashed veins

My love has knitted a blood-jumper
from your veins
which I'll wear all my life
underneath
for this jumper gives me warmth
and chill and flesh.
Her blood-jumper is so
beautiful that no one knows
it's made of blood.

So no one stares at me in dread
Because I'm wearing a jumper of blood
when I have nothing on but her blood-jumper.

Stunned by its beauty
they ask me where I got it from
'we want one just like it'
Or maybe 'could we borrow it'.

But I cannot let anyone
lay a hand on her blood.

Translated by Marina Sofia

52 Hz in Space

I could describe one evening I spent with my friend
when instead of music we listened
to the sounds of space recorded by NASA
the white noise of stars the light particles swallowed
by dark matter a spacecraft recreating
the tactile sensation that a sound leaves on your skin
there where you think nothing exists but
void silence and death we listened first to the sun
then to one of Jupiter's moons
the rings of Saturn a few of the closer stars.
But I no longer wish to describe one day
you will perceive my silence as something else
I linger among them and think of myself
& the 52 Hz song of the loneliest whale in the world
who may not be all that alone
if I were a musician I'd start my song with that
because it is out of this world
my silence could travel for years till it would be heard.

Translated by Marina Sofia

Cosmic Dust

I don't understand this world at all
nor the other one. Stellar explosions

however hard I try
how can the sun from a distant galaxy
warm me now with that hedgehog's heart
on the pavement still beating
my bicycle chain has fallen off
and I cannot put it back
cannot move on

space probes discovering
flickering alien messages
that somewhere far in the distance
there may be favorable conditions
for other forms of life

our expanding universe
our ever-growing sorrow
could we not create something more beautiful
a morning dewdrop shower
on the silver birches

when we kissed I went back to my childhood
drinking milk straight from the churn
running in the yard with white a moustache
stupidly happy – sucking on pork scratchings
doing backflips among the chicken
curtseying to the turkey

stupidly happy – when in winter your tongue
freezes on the door handle
till spring spreads mirabelle jam on your tongue

frost flowers slipping all the way
to the Milky Way

the stars were nothing more than cheesy puffs
stuck to the roof of my mouth
your morning lips hot and expectant
supernovas in the hot oil in the frying pan
a bacon omelet more beautiful by far
than any exploding stars

each pancake executed a pirouette
in the air, like a circus acrobat
or trapeze artist doing the salto mortale
with no safety net
caught perfectly – stupidly happy –
in the frying pan

when we caught butterflies in our hands
or the dough we kneaded with gran
for our homemade bread on the hearth
our fingers full of cosmic dust

you may have forgotten but there were mornings
when our blankets were radioactive
when we could not get enough of happiness
when you could not get enough of slumber
and begged for five more minutes

if you were with me now I wouldn't change a thing
not even 'five more minutes'.

Translated by Marina Sofia

Red Skies

All my thoughts have now turned
to this red dawn
like no other dawn before it
if you take out your camera
you'll see the sky in the picture
is like no sky of ours
it cannot be shared
that is all and it might be enough
if there were something to add to it.

Translated by Marina Sofia

Veronica Ștefăneț

little girl blue

the gps goes crazy
in a strange city
it tangles me through neighborhoods
as if the chaos from the interior wasn't enough
i sit on the curb
a blue arrow trembles on the map

Translated by Andreea Iulia Scridon

Promises

when the plane crashes — I make promises to the air
generous and inspired
but i land again
I squeeze through the seats and get out the door
the words remain glue to the bull's eye
they follow me into the airport building
they tickle the nape of my neck
they cling to me until the first shower

then I do the inventory
clothes, hopes, pairs of earrings, politics, apartments
the scene from *the dreamers,* numbers, libido, flowers, alphabets
everything in a heap, without categories
i pur the gas and leave

in the cafe i choose a table near the window
i pack my mistakes as *experience*
and I send my excesses to the inscription of the milk mug that reads *stay weird*
although i would prefer to be something else
naive for example

a crow wanders before the window
at the table next to me a baby fusses in a highchair

Translated by Andreea Iulia Scridon

how nice

it is to be a grown up
to lie in the tub and stare at the ceiling for hours on end
to block people on facebook
to laugh during panic attacks
to spend your last money on flowers
when the kid's high school tax is still unpaid

it's wonderful to be a grown up
on a sunny Sunday
when you suffocate with loneliness
to be invited to two parties
and fall asleep with your face to the wall
and pick at the wallpaper

Translated by Andreea Iulia Scridon

Alex Văsieș

Puglia

We're smoking weed in front of the library, among scooters.
Roberto is friends with Marco who is friends with Mauro who is friends with me.

I don't even like weed; I no longer feel any sadness from it, just space.
But they left me alone with Roberto, who was drinking beer yesterday morning at
    9:00, in the reading room.

It smells of garlic and Moschino.
Where is Mauro? Did he go for coffee?
It's the end of autumn, but the light of spring tricks the seasons.

A hundred meters further, the carabinieri smoke and hoist their machine guns on
    their shoulders.
With olive-green eyes, with olive-oiled chins.

It's that moment after lunch when all communication falls apart.
The cold, dry air makes us feel good. We want to be better
and right now I like the passage of time because I like time.

Andrea takes me by car and we go to the Ukrainian girl, Karolina or Karola.
Her boyfriend owns a house in Polignano and we sit in the sun like green parrots.

It's an invasion. They break the bark with their strong beaks, leaving the fruit shell
    on the branches.
Like us, they are crazy about almonds but can be satisfied by any kind of fruit.

In November, orange leaves float on the pool water.
Those who know how to swim swim among them and falter.

I fall asleep under long, expressionist shadows.

So where's the boyfriend? I get up from the lounger and still can't see him anywhere.
I love girls who were born with the sadness gene.
I play games with them on the PlayStation, and I go down. Down. Down. Down.

Daniele played water polo, but did not want to be an Olympic medalist.
Everyone is trying to be seen, but there in the water I wanted no one to see me.

I cried like never before.
Then I broke away and retired.
At 16, I said this was the end of my sports career.

Depression is very difficult... Do you want cocaine?
Imagine that you are the sun that fills the sky and everything around you melts.
I want to think a little before answering you.

Claudia is moving – a heat wave in December.

The explosion of the ultraviolet lamp terrifies me.

She knows what she's doing.
She opens her mouth, speaks in a low voice, but remains motionless, close to her
     pronunciation.
It's the only way she knows how to talk about it. She is aware of her lips moving and
     she likes it, she likes how her lips move, just like a dog left without water.

It hurts to look at her.
She kept a story in her chest, but the sea of forgiveness in which a complicated being
     swims blurs her, silences her.

Soon there will be no more movies, no radio drama, no clever cars, no clever people.
What nonsense, who makes you talk like that?
Nobody, but I heard you crying and I couldn't stand aside.

In the first scenes I had a shaved face; but here I wear a beard and try to speak Italian.

And what about all those people who live in the dark and don't even realize it?
It is no longer a novel or a story, a hermetically sealed villaggio in the center of a fire, in the wall of the house across the street.

It is evening in the month of our adoration.
It was only about you, from day one.

When I hear someone who knows how to speak, I free myself from my senses; like when I was at the drive-in and a guy suddenly appeared whispering in my ear.
And his voice sounded asleep, from afar, from a wet car.

A gesture without consequence, a little star on the sand.
They're not aphrodisiacs, they're a good night's sleep, i.e. awesome.

What I forgot to draw from her or his answer: the ocean.
Nothing about the darkness. Almost nothing about the darkness. Not a word about the darkness. About darkness itself.

You are silent and calm, more like a constellation.

My mind is filled with things I can't come to terms with.
And the cheetah still scratches the planet. Someone is singing St. Augustine in the blue bedroom.

Where do you eat the best focaccia barese in the world?
On this beautiful stadium, where Răducioiu once smiled and no one plays anymore.

Nothing is really great when you receive it all at once. On the boy's face and around his ankle.
And they all just look at the sky, at the twins' rainbow.

The government will give them the bad news.
Port workers got used to them.

Soon, this place will be the same as before.

A painful party.
Andrea holds Clara in his arms, I would give anything to be one of them.

The terrace only holds their eyes.

From the sea, the smell of frittura mista.
I could move here, dedicate myself to the climate, to the octopuses.

I'm as good as the things I replace.

But the stars are gone, the air is cold and hard as mud.
The air is dangerous. Nobody wears warm clothes.

Translated by Cătălina Stanislav

Hackers at the shore

Sparkling brighter than the beam moving on the screen,
their script will wash the world.
They touch rolling on the blanket,
the margins don't bleed out.
It's Python + Java + Perl,
when you lick her breasts and put two fingers in,
and it's much more,
it's the disc cracking.
Processing.
The translation of information that you push toward excess,
and corporality.
Blinking together like a little light
which develops into unity.
Where nobody can lift them,
this script — the world lacks interrogation
and primary keys.
The river flows on, infected,
it has the sound of a cooler.
After errors and several binaries,
she masturbates with her feet-
Their first sample.
Then an IP generator which opens the little gate.

Translated by Andreea Iulia Scridon

Why are you sad on May 2nd?

We've been traveling for who knows how many hours through an impossible yellow
     fog and all you say is "If you love me you have to do something."

You thought I'd want to fly over the lake, forgetting how much I hate airplanes, alt-
     hough I told you this even when Grimes gave birth.
I hate planes to the sky and back.

Your friend's uncle is afraid to take off in the fog and invites us to his place out of
     shame.
He shows us scale models and serves us an aged wine under the vine.

You wouldn't drink because nobody's allowed to drive your car.
You're so cute when you don't get what you want, especially how the yellow t-shirt
     changes you: an angry little boy with narrow shoulders.

We're toasting to me.
This is an Archangel, and she's a Tiger Wasp.
His wife, from Piatra Neamţ, bought it, and the memory makes him bite his lips in
     pain.

Here we are still together and we love each other; then why do you suddenly have a
     tear on your cheek?
You look at the sky, it's from the vine.

It's crying, the pilot tells us, his mind empty and inconsolable.
He says it a few more times, as if we don't understand.
For three years now, left alone with the planes, he repeats things until the world
     abandons him.

You stop at the farm with solar panels and start crying for real.
The desires once inside your body are now swirling around us.

Here you are still a teenager and you don't think too much about the future, alt-
     hough you think with great care about the past.

I see the moon in the rearview mirrors, over houses with lights on.

Some shine, even though the family went out to look at the stars.
Tonight, the fog holds them together.
You fall in love with the parents of the one you love, with their house, with their animals, with their set of topics, without which they would die in a conversation.
And this holds you closer to him than love.

At night, I sleep very little and sleep away from you.
The sound of you peeing soothes me, almost putting me back to sleep.
I feel the sadness in my cunt, but love is more subtle than the body.

In the morning, I see you in the garden watering three rows of strawberries; you call them Anger, Abandonment and Dedication.
I give you money, lots of money, so you don't use those kinds of words anymore.
You tell a story, but only the bees bumping against your cheek can hear it.

You always want people to think you're happy, like when sparkling water tickles your throat and nose.
The leaves tremble under the sprinkler, thanking you for the care.

Do you remember how you cried at the farm with solar panels?
Horrible.
The easiest way out of the story is to be absorbed in its tragic formula, in the universal myths of animals.

If water moves left and right, white light decomposes into its spectrum.
And I don't care how you behave in this world, I care about you, about the way the climate suits you or not.

Only when the electricity in the air makes you tremble, you realise it got cloudy.
You smile.
Seriously, so I watered in vain.

But the silence you speak in, the resignation that the sun will not rise today, that it warmed you exactly as much as you needed.

You don't even say it to me, and that's why I find it unforgettable.
It's the moment when I like you the most and I feel my heart melting.

I am saddened by loneliness as a form of criticism,
I am saddened by your cherry red windbreaker on the basalt sky,
by dreams with many people, my attention span unable to contain you.
It saddens me that I could relive this all again and that I can't want it anymore.

Translated by Cătălina Stanislav

Big fingers

The sun won't let you work and throws you into a world of sex and suffering.
She watches you and waits, although you are now in the bad part of life, where it's
    clouded,
but not raining yet, like when she laughed before she looked at the ground.

You wait for her to leave so you can wash your hands and masturbate in the trailer,
but you'd like her to stay a little longer, to shift her eyes on your swollen fingers.
If you feel sorry for someone, you don't let them jerk off crying in front of a poster.

What if you held her and soiled her bleu ciel suit.
Does it mean sky blue?
Cloudy, although not raining and the sky wasn't blue at all this month.

So she would walk all day with your marks on her back, so she'd pick up
the little one from swimming class and the instructor wouldn't look at her ass.
How many of the people you're thinking of have this problem?

She waits for you and you lose your focus too fast; you can't remember what she
    wanted from you.
You wipe your upper lip of sweat, it tastes like pollen and you're just like her now
without realising, when you lost your concentration and it started raining.

In the Rodna Mountains, in the storm, you saw blue moths raised by ants.
You named the smallest one that sat on your oily fingers Amalia,
because it had the unease of her eyes. Amalia, I must crush you. Or you me.

You're afraid machines will replace you.
You and the men swarming around, offering filters and plates and turbines.
But you'll die underneath an X5 before that 16 inch rims, light alloy.

It must be comforting – to be ripped from the world like this, not seeing a thing,
not hearing a thing. A pill of light in a glass of darkness.
Just like when she whispers, "You do as I say" and you want to laugh.

Translated by Cătălina Stanislav

Gabi Eftimie

I pretend to be a tourist in my own city
and go to the last stop.
On autopilot it doesn't take too long and the filter
disappears.
Soon, I get to the last stop. The electrified hair
has extended towards where I am going. I gather
the crumbs left by the others and try to
guess: bread, biscuits, falafel? Ahead of me there is the
"park: the city's green lung".
In the deepest depth, the fish chain onto one other,
they last like uranium.
The raven's cawing fades out.
The common loon throws its scream on the water's surface like a
fisherman's net.
I let myself fall prey to stimuli. Guided meditation.
The park has turned its sounds off, lost in time and
space, too.
At this hour, only the pigeons coo
their mantras.

Translated by Andreea Iulia Scridon

not lyricism and darkishness

I chose a place in the middle of the sun,
green beetle,
a shard of glass on my arm,
a woman dried out like a prune
crochets ahead of me,
they bicker.

Because of myopia, Monet. Or Manet? Whatever.
Yellowish, reddish, greenish-bluish.
The metallic choir of cranes return
in the spring
resounding with echoes in each enchanted valley.

A little fly swims in my coffee cup.
The bumblebee is shocked, after it burst into my
veranda.
Above us, the forest woodcock, *cruising by.*

Translated by Andreea Iulia Scridon

sputnik in the garden

butterflies between parentheses near the poppies,
a bus carries bicycles on its back, cutting though
the frame
the butterflies rise immediately, knock heads
the brier meticulously rubs the veranda's windows
in the upside-down world of the pond
the lacy line of the airplane crashes
in our garden

Translated by Andreea Iulia Scridon

Răzvan Andrei

Psalm 5

Beyond this bed there is the world —
Round, plump as a piglet.

Beyond this blanket there is life —
Cold, fixed and blind: a statue's heart.

And it snows. Your gaze is empty and alone
like a rest area toilet.

You have not been troubled by
Roosters in heat
Nor by the apocalyptic griffins
Sculpted by snowstorms at the corners of the universe.

And the sunrise came again —
Slanted, running late and white: a whiff of a comet.
Under the green bedsheets your essence snores
Contented, through its
Teeth.
And you purr like a kettle.

Closed up in the null eye
I salute the distance
By batting my eyelashes.

In the sky, among pulsations and supernovas,
The knee of mater bends:
"Have mercy upon us, You, beer-bellied God!"

Translated by Andreea Iulia Scridon

Psalm 6

(Variation on a theme by Richard Rorty)

What does it matter if you have only one soul, or many
Or if you're just an evolved organism?
What does it matter if you're a conscience, a moving
sand dune with thoughts
Or just an aggregate with stimulated C fibers?
In general, keep your power of wonder for yourself
Like treasured coins: truth is, like antiques, the noble faces
Rubbed off the heated metal from so much rubbing;
Wandering from one hand to another, from one pocket to another.
Aren't you surprised, you: as you are!
Try, struggle to be — always different, always braver,
always ahead of yourself:
Become an opera!
What we know doesn't matter much: and anyway the world overwhelms us
And we don't feel exactly at ease among the erudite exegeses.
Aren't you surprised, you: change the words you don't like, speak
with grammatical errors,
Imagine forgetting about cruelty and forgive! Have mercy!
The paths you take are swept away by tornados, the houses which
you live in sometimes,
Topple down and some are built again, then, ruined, fall into disrepair.
Among all these things you stand, aren't you surprised!
Baptize them with your name.
Forget objectivity, kiss them on the forehead! There are just a few moments
left before everything changes.
What does it matter that your love slipped through your fingers
What does it matter if you danced many times on tables, other people's eyes
fixed upon you,
Does it matter that you stay behind the curtain now and
the reflector lights have gone out?
Keep your capacity of wonder about you, your youthful gaze,

Even if life is or it isn't, even if identity exists or it doesn't —
Sit down where you like, bear everything, prepare
for what's to come, open yourself!

Translated by Andreea Iulia Scridon

The Apocalypse by Bill Kilgore, Pensioner

I love July mornings with their whiff of napalm,

The dawns in which sweat drips down our necks, stomachs and legs,

Oily like lube with which your two electrodes have been smeared.

You told me, slyly, that the time of my poetry is, invariably,

The after-time, the bland era which follows mating,

The petty eschaton developed on the surface of a bedsheet:

Time without tension: draining out heavily and yet stridently unimportant, second
     after second after second, as in the songs of the mehterân.

There's nothing to be done — we stay pinned to the mattress seeded like a

Field at the Nile's snout, knowing that victory, the revolution of ejaculation

Is just the photograph of happiness, a whirlwind from the pig's desired thigh

And which now, so wise and experienced, we realize we won't devour.

The passage from this world to the other is stuffed up

And the archangels' lollies have long been put in herbariums, pressed —

Here, on earth, are all the franchises of the inferno

And the aurora borealis blinks like strobe lights in an underground club:

Their reason for being is to see us shredded: not to look at ourselves.

We are the victims of an already consummated apocalypse:

There's no point in calculating our parallax under Proxima Centauri —

We won't go anywhere: this is where we croak!

Translated by Andreea Iulia Scridon

Ștefan Manasia

Elegy in February

Who is watching you sleep
Hidden behind the iron shades?
Who falls asleep last
First describing your sleep?
Who makes you breathe
Under the light of the wreck among algae
And fishes?
Who is hiding in the wall
Behind the iron shades?
Who calls the mornings
In coffee cups
Who is caressing their hair
In windows splashed with lime?
Who is kissing your mouth when you sleep
Like a dry orchid crawling with ants?
And who's tingling your toes?
Who is sharpening the violet nail against beams?
Who makes you dream the Acropolis of friendship
The spur of a giant plaster bird
Smashing everything
Electrocuting the flesh of the walnut tree?
Who is stuffing a walnut between your tongue
And palatine until the air
inside
turns sour like a tin eaten by rust?
Who is watching you sleep?
Who is sharpening the violet nail against beams?
And who is throwing you into the light?

Translated by Clara Burghelea

When YOU come

When YOU come
and the moon sticks
hieroglyphs on your face

when YOU
walk back home
carrying horribly heavy bags

and behind you
the firm lights up its neons
and the owner
Says *bye* to the doorman and leaves

when YOU come back home again
with heavy bags
with an empty
and mean soul
like the coltsfoot flower

paralyzed by emotion
I forget
to kiss your hand

I watch you unzip
your tall boots
I forget to take your black coat
and hang it on the peg

nicely, like a cannibal
I waited for you
a whole afternoon at the house

like others waited on a grassy bank

for the death
of the one we have always hated
(a father or maybe a mother)
what do we care

smiling
all along
in a Darwinian & comfortable way
trying to pull down
the zipper
that won't give in

We will sneak our lives
in the poem the way others passed
their sins through the needle's eye –
I whispered.
then, little girl, then I sang to you anew:

When YOU come back home again
with heavy bags
with an empty
and mean soul
like the colt shoot flower

Translated by Clara Burghelea

poem

today I felt old for the first time
after watching Pollack's movie *Bobby Deerfield*
it has been a while since I felt
real love
the one that makes the murals of old churches
sweat myrrh
the love that gives telenovela characters
that metaphysical air
so they become more than the jean brand,
the sweater they wear
the used epilator
the love that puts the man's aorta
like a bracelet around the clay ankle
of his Berber woman

today I felt old for the first time
my brain drained and dry
a snail's whitish shell
the sharp heels the passers-by cradle on
have darkened my skin like electric shocks

then I went out on the balcony
I smoked a lot
under the night canvas
I wished to have cried or jumped off
like one of the characters in hamsun
who could not freaking drown
in the worn-out heart sack where I then hid everything

Translated by Clara Burghelea

The Outskirts

I ran out of courage and suddenly my heart turned black.
I crossed the desolate alleys
but the local angels shrouded in rags and stinky
no longer looked at me with blue eyes

of ethyl. I ran out of courage,
I ran out of courage and the tracks smoothed
the ashram of the *Prodvinalco* souls.
They first covered in debris, then concrete,

finally, bitumen the insolently beautiful huts.
Since I no longer had the courage, I had three years,
six years ago, the bulldozers turned
Parcul Rozelor in a paradise for business men.

The tumor is laying siege to the brain of the slow town.
And the town oozes bitumen, concrete.
The tumor has anesthetized the nostrils:
the smog and lard stratosphere.

It can now quietly grow.
I am no longer a famished Oriental
but I am still sick of so many satraps
and the taxing of pensions

the sentencing of the satanist priests
and cutting back on maternity leave.
An India of the mind, the color of saffron
is all I have been lately dreaming of. Still.

Translated by Clara Burghelea

Paint it black

I have seen hands in the air
saluting the death flags,
I have seen children in line formation
walking towards the kamikaze plants.
I have heard the skull of the Sphynx
crack on the cheek of the other planet.

Here the napalm farms,
There, the thermonuclear vaudeville.
Here, the 50-year-old peace,
scarier and scarier.
There, the silence rushes
the blood to the ears.

I pull the duvet under her chubby
chin. I tiptoe into the living room.
Hide the key to the Chinese tank
in a place I will no longer find
myself.

Translated by Clara Burghelea

Mircea Andrei Florea

I put my hand over your leg
and record a vibration, then the vibration
becomes an emotion. the light hangs strands of dust in the air
when it's too much you want to escape
when information isn't enough anymore

when you think of people, I get dizzy
i'm bald, and my nails grow
i always think of a place for us
aseptic, cold, white, where we could be
more productive, vulnerable

where the silence will bring glaciers to the surface

Translated by Andreea Iulia Scridon

when I wake up, all I see is a greenish
membrane, foggy, the light eel
that winds outside the window, as if
the apartment was teleported to the ocean
or rather in one of those deep
aquariums, long unwashed, seen in the windows
of pet shops

I get up and look for you, the first time I notice
the plastified furniture, I think
that this is what you must have done too while I slept
you must have plastified and sterilized everything, I heard your
movements in my sleep, but I didn't understand

I find you with a mask on your face, you avoid
eye contact, you throw the food out
of the fridge, say you're tired
of us only eating only take-out

you're angry, but let
your artificial coolness
slow you down

when the cold sneaks under your clothes
I want to laugh

I laugh

alone, between the walls
in quarantine, I fall asleep

the temperature falls
I'm almost at the final destination

you wander from room to room, you stop

in strange positions, you're a spider, curled
up on the ceiling, now you're a rubber plant, a rhododendron
stable in your environment, now you're the mantis
who wants me to disappear

you're a natural

you're looking for a host, yesterday you were a larva, soon
you shall be prey, you're angry, but let
your artificial coolness
slow you down

flies gather around the shut mouths

your foot moves
like a captive insect
among the glass blades

I answer the phone, but I hear you through the house
you wander from room to room and I get hard. I speak in tongues
burdock, linden, couch grass, ambrosia, common yarrow

simulation with us running in the flat zone
little animals roaming the earth
cutting our ankles in stems, while corvids
clean the field under the barren sky

Translated by Andreea Iulia Scridon

George Vasilievici

George in the rain

watch it cry outside,
blue and red and friendly,
enough for us not to lose the occasion of this perfect day
when we can fight with frozen balls of tears
so big and convincing
that you could even put rocks in them.

anyway wrap up warm
so that the sadness or happiness
will not chill you to the bones
you would get sick
in either case
very quickly,
before concocting in your stomach
the usual creature of tears,

before you call me as you do every evening
for help, to put together its nose,
mouth and eyes, to put together its hands and the small buttons of his coat
sewed directly onto its skin,
before
stuffing in its mouth skies grown in genetic
laboratories.

But as usual, you put on a crazy flesh
received from your parents,
so that emotions won't pull you back
and now we pour onto its head the pot full of death,
bought from the corner shop. A solid, long-living death.

Cheap and good. With great chances of piling up
over something else.

Translated by Andreea Iulia Scridon

For the first time

The blood train stops in the station
We get off and head to town
Our red souls shine under our skin
Lighting up the future that spreads out
In every direction.

It's the first
Emotion.

We will settle down here for a while
Everyone says to himself
Upon descending from a drop
And gazing in the distance.

We'll make it here,
We'll find work,
There are no robots here,
And the clones who mate have
Fresh children.

We'll be fine and we'll forget
Where we came from.

We'll make love again
For the first time.

Translated by Andreea Iulia Scridon

The second hidden room (Fragment)

3

we find ourselves alone in a room with two rooms,

submerged, in the depths

In the middle of the unknown, like a room with two rooms

The first room was on the right and had two rooms,

The second room was on the left and had two rooms,

there are two rooms in each room. Twice

as many rooms.

And on the ceiling your coffee skies with whipped cream clouds.

Divided equally for each resident guest of the rooms.

Let them all eat the hariboo bears as an elastic

Frosting, protecting all with the jelly trampoline.

Catapulting whatever touches you. But I like to say anything.

Everything jumps in all directions now,

Flying, spreading broken wings,

You can fly better with two broken wings than

With one broken wing under some foreign skies

And this is one of those rooms where

Each room has its own skies. Two at a time,

Four at a time, eight at a time, sixteen at a time, blue at time,

Skies up to heaven and back to you.

Translated by Paul Doru Mugur

only those who don't exist have a future

everything that has passed becomes brief,
crushed and hard second
trampled by us,
steps on us

age rests.
who never lied,
let him say "I",
and, so, they will lie.

me with me and with us
we divide perfectly
by one.

everything to the end
without hesitation
and in absolute
solitude.

i don't love myself enough,
i always need someone,
to be able to see
my whole face.

I don't know how much I am and how much
there are others in me,
only the ones whose death I've seen have a specific place,
a fixed percentage.
Otherwise, only footsteps through the others
and their footsteps through me
but this road leads nowhere
it doesn't even end
I would understand the wall regardless

of its nature,
without it, the gaze does not stop,
and I wake up
far, far away!
so far from me
that I don't have time
to come back

instead of *me* we should say *au*
instead of you *we* should say *zu*.

and the tear freezes
like blood.

Translated by Paul Doru Mugur

the object collapses into the subject

I only do what I feel like doing,
now I sharpen a pencil,
and I draw with it
high buildings on my eyeballs
then I rise high up
from where I can see
the deepest inside me.

whoever wants to see me,
should look up.

whoever doesn't believe
that we can see each other clearly
when we look up,
should look up.

now that everyone is looking up,
I collapse into myself, too,
jumping from the height
drawn by my look.

In a flash, I pass through the hearts
of those that I keep in my heart
and when I touch the ground
they all draw
high buildings on their eyeballs.

Translated by Paul Doru Mugur

a hundred percent

%la%la%la%la%la%la%la%la%la
%la%la%la%la%la%la%la%la%la
%la%la%la%la%la%la%la%la%la
%la%la%la%la%la%la%la%la%la
%la%la%la%la%la%la%la%la%la
%la%la%la%la%la%la%la%la%la
%la%la%la%la%la%la%la%la%la
%la%la%la%la%la%la%la%la%la
%la%la%la%la%la%la%la%la%la
%la%la%la%la%la%la%la%la%la
%la%la%la%la%la%la%la%la%la
%la%la%la%la%la%la%la%la%la
%la%la%la%la%la%la%la%la%la
%la%la%la%la%la%la%la%la%la
%la%la%la%la%la%la%la%la%la
%la%la%la%la%la%la%la%la%la
%la%la%la%la%la%la%la%la%la
%la%la%la%la%la%la%la%la%la
%la%la%la%la%la%la%la%la%la
%la%la%la%la%la%la%la%la%la
%la%la%la%la%la%la%la%la%la
%la%la%la%la%la%la%la%la%la
%la%la%la%la%la%la%la%la%la
%la%la%la%la%la%la%la%la%la
%la%la%la%la%la%la%la%la%la
LOVE

Translated by Andreea Iulia Scridon

Cristina Stancu

unknown places where my bike breaks down on the way to jobs / side entrances of office buildings and hotels / warehouses images of traffic and objects sent to spaces where i didn't want to go / strangers eating standing up smoking next to me speaking languages i don't understand / suddenly faces / the disgusted receptionist telling me what i'll find inside / blood and used condoms / all the shades of lipstick on their pillowcases and the piles of gas containers forcing them to laugh long into the morning / the small aluminium cans a mountain then the spaces where i was afraid to speak / crossings through deserted office campuses with exhausted people smoking in the covered rectangle next to all the strong competent women telling me i'd be fine here and there / next to the buildings with rusty logos that reminded me of home / here / afraid to speak and superimposed over the image of the outdoor freezer room / the dumpster in the restaurant parking lot where extended families parked and watched / the repetitive eight-hour motions at the conveyor belt / left-right hand up-down-center / evenings when the serbian family drove me closer to my home in this foreign town where events were mere narrative tricks / we're in that weird episode where action takes place in a different time frame and / autopsies of those who lived through periods of famine during wars just proved we've understood evolution wrong / prosperity and happiness clog our arteries / just like me the fifth state of matter has properties that disappear in contact with the real world / when they will dig deep into our tissues for things of value / i wonder if they'll see i've created something so small and personal

Translated by the poet

hundreds of idiotic histories
generated daily
and if it doesn't go anywhere
why do i have to laugh:

the poem from 3 am i'll never finish
since the chair crashed to the floor.

what i did to some is hate.

(enrique baeza says reality is spam.
virginia woolf says true reality exists.
lauren e. simonutti says nothing is real
but everything is true.)

Translated by Alina Ștefănescu

the world clarifies its
irrelevance
abandonment
in the store window
good day
I'm scared of myself

(an artificial supernova goes out on the screen
i follow it with oil streaks left by a forefinger
blood type O has 37% less
chance. edit: of developing pancreatic cancer.
a finger was found in the guts of carp fished
from the lake where a man lost his finger.
edit: a body holds an immense carp in its arms
which bears a finger in its guts.)

i cut my nails right to the flesh and try not to hope
i eat less and less
so the world will be less afflicted
sometimes i think my insides are a man
that wants to be a woman

fixed frames from inside the museum after
pulverized visitors poured themselves in front of what
was exhibited in the window.
Afterwards something brownish on the floor
clotted — this is how we make history.
after staring at the recorded video
those of us from outside thought we could change
the way we hated ourselves.

(in the snowstorm outside the arab poets are executed
for poems twitter opinions and raised voices in cafes.
in the free world a ten year old girl
tries to sell her grandparents on ebay. peace.)

in the house in the middle of campus past the green fence and
the rose garden beyond the poems of ashraf fayadh
about humans and bread beyond the rapid
streetlights there are no wreaths about the dead
only unconsumed time of which
we cannot speak.

Translated by Alina Ștefănescu

when diane arbus photographed dwarf prostitutes
identical twins
with hypnotic eyes and sad lives and she loved them but did not
want it anymore.

when anne sexton lit her last cigarette and dressed in the
fur coat
inherited from the mother who accused her of triggering her cancer.
there was no one there
when sexton undressed in front of the daughters
to help them feel less.

when plath replaced my brain which
described the phenomena that makes our stomachs hurl us
(poc!pssssh!)

when david foster wallace was writing the letter
that went on for 25 pages explaining why they broke up
as she only read one page.
when david foster wallace said never to leave
a burning building.

when constantin virgil banescu whispered to the linguistic structure
resitting
why we eat spheres and i still do not know

Translated by Alina Ștefănescu

"we just woke up and for no reason we ended up
on a bench in the middle of town
at sunrise. since then i can only imagine happiness like
this – a video that doesn't load"

you focus on a fixed point and start gathering
everything you have in a corner. it doesn't matter
if they disturb you since you're in your own treatise
on symptoms. these rules describe you.

Translated by Alina Ştefănescu

kilograms of humans. kilos of humans transmitting parasites
reality show about intermittent interdictions and rebellions

(in a japanese cafe you can pay 1000 yen
to be hugged for three minutes.
the clientele pays another 1000 yen to caress
a girl's head. another 1000 if the client
gets to look into the girl's eyes for a minute)

i imagined a body kept standing by dozens of matrices
glued in equilibrium from the inside. one inside the other
a matryoshka of meat eating itself advancing towards its own center.
and at the end there was a cell which smelled of frankincense where
i needed to remain motionless.

i longed for things that
i could not write in poems while humans
were good for nothing. on the street walls between the living
i memorized the places with access to toilets
and then left. i have found addresses missing floors and
too many mornings. *now make sure no one else is coming
and hide in the closet.*

Translated by Alina Ștefănescu

when you were little
you wrote a story
about a girl
who hated herself
so thoroughly
that one day
she disappeared
and someone else
took her place.

(in december 2017 the first head transplant
will take place in china. the donor will be
a prisoner who will not consent to it.
the patient who receives the new head
will be put into an induced coma for a month
to prevent the rejection of the head
by the body.)

(silvina ocampo says that if others
imagine us dead
we'll die.)

Translated by Alina Ştefănescu

a joke says we are incurable, sexually transmitted
terminal diseases.
kids born with lobstein disease or *osteogenesis imperfecta*
live for around twenty minutes because their bones
are rotten thread. *we* can't uninstall.
for the tumor we are the cancer:

the microscopic structure of dry human tears
resembles an apocalyptic landscape. the canals dug
along the length of a territory that no longer sustains life.
some mole species rub their bodies with tears
to protect themselves from the aggression of others.
unlike them, our violence disappears
only when we believe we're the same.

Translated by Alina Ștefănescu

next to you mutilated genitals, pain, 60 days non-stop
completely destroyed uterus, umbilical cord cut with teeth
she speaks for the children because she doesn't exist

to always keep the high stakes of the moment
when i wait in line to be told
if my organs have failed

matthew mcconaughey explaining on youtube
that it's not happiness but joy

i dreamt of an infection that had become superpower
there were no more continuous currents, just outflows
repeated outpours of the same character
britney spears as a fixation of collective guilt

but look how beautifully one hell connects to another
how good we manage to be ourselves while
we wish for it to end
the amount of calm we place into the world by trying to break free

name: Amal Alshteiwi / cause of death: suicide / age: 9 years old

when the younger ones will learn how to think we will hold them
in our arms. it will be their first lesson in survival: here we cannot
be attacked if we feel safe, not even in cerebral suspension
in the chaos of cells with 2,000 electrodes in the motor cortex
or in the disgust we stir up in others

Translated by the poet

i wanted to clearly explain what it means to be the most compostable species
explain goodness until it became the ideology of the better equipped
place people under glass bells in the dark
tell them it's an art installation or maybe the screens will be hacked
and they will threaten us with our lives in real time
the christian concept of damnation has driven suicidal christina
johansdotter to kill a child in order to be executed
the original sketch of the gas chamber and crematorium resembles
the hand of a robot playing the piano
if you react the stories stop, says the priest
grief has 5 stages, decomposition only 4 because a dead body
will no longer accept anything. listen, tell yourself you're just
another symptom of disappearance
we form in layers and our feelings adapt to technology and
change their usefulness. the image of marilyn scotch-taping
the note on her stomach begging the doctor not to remove her ovaries
the house on the boulevard demolished at ground floor
but with clean curtains upstairs
even in 2017 marilyn's pelvic x-ray
was worth a small fortune people who want to see inside other people
marvel at the props needed to prove who we are

Translated by the poet

Iulia Militaru

Death: What is free of your intentions/What always occurs outward;
Reprehensible when it becomes your intention/Reprehensible when it doesn't occur
    outwardly.

 The perfect model of decentralizing,
 losing the head, the absolute freedom of the body:
1. the myocardium remains excitable for 15-20 minutes;
2. muscular fibers keep their excitability for 5-6 hours;
3. the pupil can be stimulated
(by subconjuctival injection of Atropine or Pilocarpine, for 4-6 hours);
4. the cilia from the respiratory epitelium keep their mobility for 12/24/36 hours;
5. spermatozoa keep their mobility for 72 hours.
These are the supravital manifestations,
in other words, all that is above life.

A supreme anticapitalist gesture, the gathering of capital.
 Facial hair and nails grow anarchically,
 The intestines live for the first time
 The miracle of unconditional liberation
 From the acumulated gas. Flatulence,
 The moment of great personal freedom

Death can be sold and bought on the black market for a minimum price.
Negotiation is allowed only outside the accredited institutions
    where the price is fixed and mandated by the State.

Death—not at all a sudden occurence, but a dynamic process with variable length in
    which the vital systems of the body participate simultaneously or in sequence and
    which results in the demise of the individual. This process is influenced by the
    variable response of the cells to diminishing quantities of oxygen și nutrients.

Early signs: the cooling of the body, dehydration, autolysis, deathly palor, rigor mortis.

Later signs: destructive changes caused by animals, insects, rot;

Preserving changes (through mumification, lignification, freezing, mineralization)

[Did you know... that recently, it was discovered that the dead don't rot any longer:

1st Voice: "For 20 years since I've been working as a grave digger here, I found many mummified bodies. We find one every 2-3 weeks. I remember about a month ago, when we had to dig up someone, we found a lady perfectly mummified. Her face skin was stretched, teeth in their places, even her clothes were in good condition. When we dug her out of the grave and held her up, she stood as if she were alive".

2nd Voice: "Lately, the gravediggers find more and more mummified bodies when they exhume the ones dead for over 7 years. Some say it's God's miracle, others say the tombs are to blame because they're sealed and don't allow bacteria to decompose the body. The researchers say the bodies don't "properly" rot any longer because of the preservatives and additives from the food we eat daily.

All of these signs were recently graded.

No one ever believed there is a death Law,

(let alone, a definition of it; only images)

One could die and live as they pleased:

1. Suicide by firearm, September 20, 1890, female; the following note was found:
Beloved Vasile, if you'd like to do me a last favor, please pay the washerwoman 7 lei and 50 bani; I wouldn't want her to curse my soul; and to the kerosene seller I have to pay 1 leu and 75 bani; if you want, ask the French woman or the maid to pay him. Please don't deny me my last wish. And one more thing. Please, I'm asking you, when I'm dead, show some interest in me, do something, anything you want, to show you're sorry, or do what you know, but do it so the world can see. You know very well this is not for me, because I won't know anything; but for you, because there are some people who know my predicament and they will gossip a lot behind your back. They are already, even without this. Please, listen to me, do something to save your reputation, something that wouldn't cost you any money you don't have. Please listen, I know what I'm saying. Forgive me for giving you advice, it's because I don't want you to have any troubles because of me. Kisses!

2. Suicide by poisoning with phenic acid, November 21, 1890, male; the following
   note was found: *Look, I'm drinking phenic acid; I'm poisoning myself!*

3. Suicide by poisoning with arsenic, December 11, 1898, unspecified sex; no note
   was found; in the morgue archive's log, one can read: *He didn't say he was sick
   with anything; but for a while this person was very sad.*

More abuse occured.
Denying death, overvaluing life,
the absence of a clear explanation for
being alive.

Lastly, the ultimate confusion.

Epode: They resorted to SCIENTIFIC/research.

T(a/o)[u/n](a)thology: The study of all aspects related to death/Is called tanathology.

The experiments were developed
in several stages:

1. Decorporalization (exiting the body, perceiving events that occur farther away
   from the individual)
2. Increasingly fast aspiration through a tunnel at the end of which one can see an in-
   tense but gentle light; along the way, the individual replays the entire life.
3. Before merging with the light source, the individual returns to his/her body (the
   return is extremely unpleasant)

The results were analyzed,
Solid counterarguments were made
Against the proof of "after life" existence:
- *The existence of an universal halucination prototype, regardless of cause (tiredness, fever,
  epilepsy, drugs, sensory deprivation)*
- *Very similar phenomena can occur through electrostimulation of the temporal lobe in
  the fissure of Sylvius or through administering ketamine, phencyclidine, or LSD*

- It's possible that these sensations are caused by massive endorphins production.

A law, to regulate this aspect,
toxic for any developed society, was necessary.

Elaboration: A few capable individuals were needed.
They gathered two-three words,
Placed them in a certain order,
Constructing meaning. Then, they priced it.

1ˢᵗ Epode: So any Law can be/is sold. The one who doesn't own a Law should buy
   one!

This is the role of the parliament: to sell us overpriced laws,
otherwise known and accepted by the citizens as a parliamentary salary.

A law can be good or bad. To select the good ones,
fit for commercial purpose, we need a president.
His advice cost also a considerable amount of money.

The process of selling and buying laws is called democracy.
For this, democracy is not necessary; only the capitalist spirit is a must.

2ⁿᵈ Epode: Any spirit can in turn be/is sold.
   The one who doesn't have a spirit should buy one!

Commercial break/time rotation:

Because the SPIRIT is your guardian,
Any herd (of well-tempered domestic animals), in its absence, is vulnerable.

He, known as the shepherd,
"accepts to take on his shoulders the animals' sins, so they don't have to pay a price";
the shepherd will be the one who pays a price,

instead of you. This is the advantage of being shepherded!

Results: According to the Law, it was established that:
Total death = the end of activity of all the body cells

The Law's contradictions:
It's not clear if "death" means:
1. cardiac activity arrest (?)
2. the irreversible destruction of the brain (?)

Positive diagnostic of cerebral death:
1. complete loss of relation life
2. total muscular areflexia and atonia
3. BP drop when the iatrogenous support is cut off
4. spontaneous respiration stop
5. persistent electrical "quiet" on the EEG

There are people that can stay in a vegetative state several years and who
spontaneoulsy recover their cerebral activity.
Because of the existence of cerebral death, the confusion between living and non-
living persists, which makes applying the law difficult.

Several amendments were necessary.

Exclusions from the "Living" category after imposing the definition and establishing the death legislation

So far we don't have all the necessary approvals to cite a complete list.

On the short list, there are noted only:
1. The category of the one who believes himself the father of the next two categories,
proudly calling himself "the author"; at this one, it was observed, in time, the
presence of the signs necessary to maintain the diagnostic of cerebral death, in
other words, of the irreversible destruction of the brain: first and foremost, the

complete loss of relation life, areflexia, and thepersistent electrical "quiet" on the EEG.

2. The category of the one that history thought innofensive up to a point, but was wrong: "the reader"; his death through cardiac arrest was necessary. Besides the cooling of the body, lividity, and rigor mortis, he started to show destructive changes caused by insects and rot. Each reader has a specific stench. But miraculously, it was observed that the spermatozoa retained their mobility, in this type of body, even after more than 72 hours since death. Thus, the reproductive function continues to develop well. So far, science couldn't plausibly explain this phenomenon.

3. The "poem"category: with ambiguous signals from this category, such as, firstly, the absence of a deceased body, it is believed the poem has been hiding in a vegetative state for several years, and everyone is feverishly awaiting its spontaneous revival.

Epode: It's worth mentioning the fact that none of the excluded categories is definitely excluded.

Exclusion oscillates depending on the historic period and context. *Everything is relative.*

Additional specifications regarding death

If interested in the faith of its members, society will be announced of their death through an obituary published in the pages of the local papers.

A beautiful omage, sometimes touching, demonstrates everyone's interest at a very low price. Following are a few examples of such obituaries, copied from the journal of my grandfather, Ion Popescu:

1. *Toward the end of March 1953, Iosif Visarionovici Stalin (aged approx. 73 years) passed away. At that time, our country kept three days of mourning, and church bells rang everywhere for him. That's when I heard that many party members were confused by the bells, since communists are atheists and don't believe in God.*

2. *In the year 1978, I found out from the newspaper România Liberă that reserve colonel Elefterescu Juarez has passed. I went to his funeral at the Resurrection cemetery where*

I met several reserve officers that I knew and spent some time talking with them. Also from the newspaper România Liberă I found out that the following have passed:

* Barat Israel (Liviu), former major and my boss at the M.I. A.;

* Onviceanu Emil, former chief of the fridge shop at the Repairs Group

* Bârlădeanu Vasile, former colleague of mine at the Endowments Ministry.

3. *In the newspaper România Liberă from May 14, 1978, they announced the sudden passing of the singer from Dâmbovița County, Ileana Sărăroiu. She was buried on Wednesday, May 16, at the Sfânta Vineri cemetery.*

4. *In the newspaper Flacăra from September 13, 1979, no.37, a very important article was published: "The Ranitescu Inheritance", by dr. res. col. Ranitescu Dumitru, deceased on September 2, 1979 (operated in July 1979). He had created the product D.R. that cures a series of cancerous diseases. Death occurred through an accident not yet explained (under investigation); (text written by Emanoil Valeriu).*

5. *On Sunday, February 22, 1981 reserve colonel Bârsăşeanu Cristache was buried at the Crângaşi cemetery. I couldn't attend because I went to the public bath in Giuleşti.*

6. *In the newspaper România Liberă from November 12, 1986, it was announced that Viceslav Molotov, former politician in Stalin's time, has died at 96 years of age.*

7. *Tuesday, January 13, 1987, three years since Edi's death, Rica kept a requiem at the cemetery. She also paid for an obit in the newspaper România Liberă in which it was written:* On January 13, three years since the sudden stop of the thread of many happy years, when I lost forever the wise, kind, and honorable man, engineer Eduard Rădulescu, former director in the Labor Ministry. Now I know only the pain, longing, and the suffering of terrible loneliness until the end of my life. — Wife Maria

8. *Tuesday, June 23, 1987, it was published in the newspaper România Liberă that colonel engineer Nedeianu Jakues, who was my boss at the Construction Service from the M.I.A., has died. When I retired on March 1, 1977, he sent his secretary to buy for me: a robe, a pair of slippers, and a bottle of wine of the best quality. I was sorry I couldn't go to the funeral.*

9. *In the România Liberă newspaper from Friday, July 10, 1987, it was published that father Munteanu from the Crângaşi church has died, and in the paper România Liberă from July 14, 1987, it was published that resrve colonel Ursache Dumitru, who worked with me at the M.I.A.,[9] has died.*

10. *In the România Liberă newspaper from July 30, 1987, it was published that Gheorghe Petrescu, great stateman, the brother of Elena Ceauşescu, born in May 1915 in*

---

[9] M.I.A.= Ministry of Internal Affairs

the village of Petreşti, Dâmboviţa county, has died. In the same newspaper it was published that army general Ion Ioniţă, aged 64, has died.

Epilogue

after Anemone Latzina

Dear Anemone, don't give up!

As for him…

He broke countless windows, exhausted by too much patience
and tasted hungrily from your bodies, like a hyena.

Alone, he surrounded himself with thick walls, so you can't watch him.
But one morning, he found himself in your orchard full of fruits.

He sent several people to their death while they were kissing his body,
so joyously, as no one ever was.

Then he made love in the sea, despite its coldness,
he made love there, until four blond children were born.

Now, drunk on too much absinthe, he looks to the end of all five,
Killed by life's small illusions he weaves impatiently for them.

He desired the pleasant drug sweetness each day,
and, in this dream, he replated the scented date trees from your garden.

He won ten medals for this, plus countless riches,
then, he started shooting cats with golden bullets.

Sometimes, he danced the polonaise so well in your arms,
But, unknowingly, he fell in love on May 13 and forgot.

Suddenly, he saw himself inside, and the ones outside returned.

Sometime, maybe by accident, I'll commit suicide, as well.

Laughing.

But… what is important is the end of a form[10]
The more free you are, there is only suicide, even when
your death is declared to have occured by natural causes.

Now you understand the Werther effect?

DEATH – *the condition of life progress!*

Translated by Claudia Serea

---

[10]The bodies can be:

buried (in soil, in caves, in tree hollows, in funeral wells, in monumental graves),

incinerated, exposed to open air, thrown into rivers, or eaten in ritualic endocanibalism, etc.

Monica Stoica

like a breath of fresh air in all this chaos

fog just fog and mold and laughter in the bar.
we left the 10 degrees weather to be somewhere anywhere
just inside. somewhere under the wind
i was thinking about your eyes, -like a gust of wind, you wrinkle
The World
swallowed us with her abstract whirlwind
of emotional ammunition and recognizable shapes
and teenagers swallowed us with cigarette smoke
from before the start of the university term.
there were three more days and the year tilted towards October.
they had no birch vodka at the bar, the kind you drink.
and to me they gave a glass of wine filled to the brim.
it was a kind autumn. the wind howled like a dog in
heat.
when you kissed me for the first time the girls had gotten drunk
and played Bobby Vinton on the speakers his teenager
voice
Blue Velvet and the natural red-head, Ana's mouth
so fleshy her body, her boobs, her moldavian
accent.
how you would have liked to fuck her, sweetheart.
we changed the subject, we talked about God
the brain of men and dolphins.
what could be said about the night:
a mist of grace covers the smokehouse
you felt the fluid composition of the night.
and told me: too many people around. so many brains
per square meter

vibrations and you, what texture do your lips have?
he blinded me, he tore me to shreds
– a very human feeling. very exact.
like a breath of fresh air in all of this chaos –

Translated by Iarina Albu

ultimatum game

after the dream with the photographic reproduction that seemed more real
than reality

    i tried to remember why you also dreamt of
apartments in ruins
pipes peeking out of the walls, old ladies in rags that had already stolen
your soul,
who and why would need to use this much energy, lucidity and
youth,
who is there to plant black flowers under your bed, as in the book
of spells,
who told you that reality is quantified and that we
don't even know
who's pulling the strings, how do you know that people that do
black magic are like a luxury tomb, reek of rotten meat and roses,
they burst with money,
how do you know you can only think of one thing
at a time,
that the demon sleeps in your bed. and how can we
tame evil, if
the demon looks in your dream like a rabid goat, like a crocodile
that chews on my hair.
one day we'll run into each other.
behind us the city will be evicted.
we'll look for keys in the mud with our crumpled-up hearts
undetected by the social security services
and suddenly that's where they will stop.

Translated by Iarina Albu

crushed next to the technodrome

magnetized and motionless, we will touch again
under interdiction,
in deathly vapors, crushed under technology, insanity and
biological death,
what else is there to do? next to us there will be astral people
awoken spiritually
like a 24/7 supermarket always open and well lit. what will we do,
absorbed by the last
flicker and by the last prayer of human effort to
fit into this immunologic
space where everyone has already injected the antidote?
but us.

Translated by Iarina Albu

oh, baby, baby

the scent of jasmine was still intact in my room.
i was crying; hazy hours stringed together.
/ we're humanoids living in these time
gaps /
the musical background is exactly right, a whining doo-wop.
with a jump in time, a jump in space,
we're squinting out a motel window in 1960's America,
right when the juke box breaks.

the flies invade the empty dance floor
and the jasmine pots in the windows.
they sit on the freshly washed wood of the floor.

Translated by Iarina Albu

This puts my brain in overdrive

what were you saying, M., about the brain,
the fibonacci cat was wriggling on the floor,
your post-apocalyptic wallpaper,
the shiny robot
meant
the end of rational perception
the start of sensuality
because
the explosive, balsamic beauty of your hands,
put my brain in overdrive.
and the lines of code you wrote with such elegance
impregnated on my catatonic figure
were knitting the fuchsia comic book
background of that sunset.
i moved my fingernails slowly, in a line on your back
our tongues desperately searching each other
in that porno night.

beyond you the cherry blossoms fell in imponderability.
the blackbirds whispered endlessly in my ears.
your brain lit up in the dark.

Translated by Iarina Albu

sexual healing

transitory surge. the folliculin screams on the sidewalk.
there where the girl with the cap walks, big boobs and electric
nipples, the blonde with braces, gleaming with desire
the boy in the white shirt with perfect vascularization. it's
time to check the app. we'll discover the source
of the transitory surge, we'll take our gadgets and with
a locomotory force we'll leave the town where traffic lights
change too fast before you can cross (remember
the precocious sexuality?) (remember the frigidity?)
(remember the desire and the act itself?). the latest a.i.s
should talk about psychotherapy. online, on
the chat, sms, in hysteria, in decline. last night, however, a few people
dreamt of a woman with amnesia. she didn't even know what the act itself
was. which of us tried at the same time to do
bukkake, to lick, to suck, to love like a pro,
in the era of seriousness and overinterpretation? someone
speaks of the transitory surge and maybe
it's a conspiracy and what intensity when the mystical syntagm
has the prefix ,over-' and is volatile. on the t-shirts of men
is written mannschaft. day after day mortal kombat in the city. but
the heart has fuel and tension leaks. in the bedroom
the bodies became cyanotic. on the road, uphill,
hungry birds devour ringed
worms.

Translated by Iarina Albu

the animalic darkness inside us has a retro sound

although you were in an urban environment, riddled with social convention
you had fallen from the Moon. you had been mean to me. one night you
told me: 'if i hadn't seen you today, i would never have seen you'. you, with
no worries. although you had the possibility to fade the fuck away
the despair, although there was the possibility of an orderly life.
you were laying in a mined field, apocalyptic. it was the way you were. or
not. maybe it's just perceptions, voluntary distortions, what
i often see when i dream, the cities after conflagrations and dogs
forgotten on the sidewalk in the cradle of the day. my feelings have
a bullet effect – straight to the heart. maybe i see through photocromic lenses
when actually you're a primary, grave, sober color, like
an imminent tragedy. it might have just been a contrast. the black
sky, you, white as foam, what's with you, when the butterflies in your belly
die there, in your belly? what do you want, with your feminine diamond
mind and a vacation in the isle in my head? you want my heart,
my soul, my body? when the world is a tiny black
dot and all the philosophies about the animalic darkness
inside us have a retro sound. this girl is fragile and eats snow out of
your palm if it snows. she eats dirt with a teaspoon if
you ask her to. this girl looks at you and sniffs you out. and you how do
you manage all this? how do you take it? it's night and from time to
time a ray from the lampposts severs the night.
i miss you with a supersonic force that's all the rage, an
armored concoction, it traverses over the buildings
and its black box belongs to you.

Translated by Iarina Albu

Florentin Popa

miklagaard

far, far away from the Maidenskeep hilltop
where the asphalt starts curling around its edges
like bandage on a breast
after you pass that house decked in solar panels
and its denizens, eating thick jam, trading ethereum
and taking a jolly, sovereign, self-determined piss
right on their porch

three miles away from any remnants of the material plane
where not even the aroma of Lidl pretzels
can reach them in the morning
far away, towards he village of Tăuți
where they still put out the fires in their hearths with whey
far, far away — the fields reveal their ashen cheeks
burnt cottages for moles
the church with crows instead of tiles
and then roughly six millimeters further
'till one gets stuck in the endless thistle brambles
where deer and doe are prancing
weaving on their hooves
bleating *ohshitmate I almost got stung*
stretching in the distance as far as the eyes can see
so that, at one point, your eyes would be like
man, is there more beholding to do?
bounded by a cliff, resting like
a drunk man's jaw against the table

just a little bit further
lays hidden a valley full of plum trees in bloom
a broad and sticky furrow in the clay
like a stab through a linen shirt
and not much else

and if the servers are kind enough not to go down
like spent cicadas tapping on their sycamores
and if we are kind enough not to collapse
like ants, exhausted by their flight and mating
if only the seas are merciful
headsets for two, hands sandwiched in a close grasp

I'll take you there

Translated by the poet

anahata

I'll tell them: "I don't hate you *all that much*"; endorse
their leaning on my shoulder with a drunken whiff
I'll bring them bags of cheese puffs, I'll caress them if
they're purring; still do that when they unsheathe their claws

karuna and metta wisecracking; I might leave
the same sea slowly lapping at my toes, at her toes
we'll share buses and trains; passing time, huddled close
and — though righteous at last — sniff when they feel quite stiff

and I'll hold everyone in the grasp of my palm
icicles-become-fingers — like those fingers were mine
and I'll rebuke my heart: please be still, please be calm

and keep my hand from freezing when I see them shine
then melt in midwinter 'till they're completely gone —
water still holding warmth, yet none of their design

Translated by the poet

the sadness

I have seen things you would not believe
helicopters chopping away at the moonlight
children gently touching the burn marks on their shoulders
naked inside derelict staircases
bathed in chlorine and lasers beaming from afar
shining forth from the goa plastic-pillared temple
of our holy mother of the midnight
and I've seen Shiva in their midst, but nothing of them in shiva
spirals collapsing back into spirals

I have seen it all glued to my chair
hand on my mouse in a Nosferatu grip
before the internet got consolidated into four websites
back when it was much more like a CRT screen,
back when it was 10 times warmer, 10 times more capricious
back when it used to mostly deliver
porn for ants and friends from far away

and I have seen Sadness slapping its wristwatch
just like Ben10 used to — under raven kaleidoscope heavens
I'm just a girl who's stacking up canned tuna — half asleep —
on supermarket shelves all packed with lindt
chocolate, resting her head on her shoulder
her cheeks draped in weird absinth
blush, singing along with the voice in her headphones
so dreamily yet barely getting the gist
I got that summertime summertime sadness
spirals collapsing back into circles — with us in their midst

and I have seen your sadness
descending through underground passages
late at night, through huge pipelines dripping at their joints
like old people sitting up — at the end of their beds

in the middle of the night — frozen solid in their gloom
your sadness like a gang of schoolboys fighting
dragging their feet through hoarfrost
holding hot donuts in at least one hand
kicking each other in the shins — somewhat careful not to drop them
sadness no. 7 when the night is hurtling towards monday
grabbing the magic by the neck, pushing its head in a pillow
and scattering its brains — like an angry cat in a litter box
sadness no. 31 when all you want
is someone okay to be sad around
    and yet it's simply not possible
151 new and exciting varieties of sadness
now in their shiny version *you gotta catch them all*

I've seen the nth and umpteenth reruns
cliché ante-prequels post-sequels part three
of that movie of us collapsing back into me
and there is no one no-no-no there is no one
no-one left in my midst. but you see
this summer will drop dead
one thursday. these moments — grapes burnt together
with dead leaves, on the vine — tears we shed
amidst rain fractals will be lost in time
and longing and unending, and free —
these black waves with no tether

Translated by the poet

pashupati 2

this tomcat licking his wound as if it were
a strawberry ice cream in the feather-grass
then sneezing — his eyes asquint — greenish ravines
right under; fairy flies falling apart even
when gently blowing air towards them; this cat
is neither running scared, nor is he arching
his soft spine as though an invisible hand
would have picked him up; but calmly stands his ground
flexing his paw — like anime heroes do
when *shonen* characters acquire eerie
fingerless, glowing gloves — then proceeds to drag
a short Capri Sun straw away from a snail
just lying there, half crushed, close to a blue shard
of tri-coloured ROM chocolate plastic wrapping

and then I squat — and we allow each other
to dwell a little longer: I — in the light of
his bone-softening torpor (like sativa
at monday morning tea) while he's in my shade
my sunken-eyed dark circle wearing shadow
as though I'd leave it here, distraught — and would then
head to some other place: *a try-catch-error*
the narrow slits of star-devouring eyes
back to the place where time had defeated light
these all-embracing, yet non-discerning eyes:
two square-jawed gigachads stuck in a narrow
hallway — too tight to fit both of them — in their
pectoral workout day at the gym, greeting
each other: "*mmm you're looking mighty fine, king*"

and then we carry on — one past the other
not without him grazing ever so slightly
(honest mistake) an atom's worth of tail

against my ankle. not without me thinking
of his life of hardships: burrs stuck to his fur
dew freezing on his whiskers while he's resting
his heart — always just a few inches away
from the ground; secret and ecstatic paths
lit by the pheromones — fluorescent lilies —
under his nostrils, nettle and mint that twist
his drooling body stretching in the sunlight
making him oblivious just for a while
to the ruby smears, the traces of fresh blood -
I hope you're thinking about me, mister cat

about my scent: of home and of another cat
my panting and my belt squeezing me harder
about how all of us — the dudes of this world
could be like this in every single moment
joined in our silent approval — *namaste*
earnestly bearing, purring in our suffering
about me merely saying I've *got* sadness
and how it doesn't have to mean I *am* sad
about this ashen circle and the one key
typing us full of typos. the fear of death
the radiant lotus that's holding it inside
where did it come from? why does it not subside
this pain — a green apple cut across its breadth
when I'm so bad at showing what's good in me?

Translated by the poet

T. S. Khasis

OK?

OK
God doesn't exist
Satan doesn't exist
It's only us
Babbling on about God and Satan
And our new cars and our Facebook posts
About conscience and freedom and money
About islands
We'd love to live on
Retreat to with the illusion of healing. And there
Dwell on one or two childhood memories
Such as the taste of crème brûlée.
Just us trying to reveal now and then
The nonsense flitting through our mind
Which we want to be amazing
Just us with our failures
Just us in our homes
Supremely intangible on the edges of the Milky Way
Which we stop to 'like' every so often

To think it's worth it
What a con
No matter what

Now we have to mimic
An irresistible force in a gift box tied with a ribbon
Deliberately left
At the door

What a useless present
Not thrown – oh no! –
Carefully carried, weighed, judged
In some way or another
More important – in the moment –
Than anything we need to say
With that politeness we all know
Is merely politeness.
More important than the clear ring
Of the doorbell

The change
Every time
Is so sudden
Costs me so much –
You think I don't know?

I make no plans
Which of course isn't the right way
But I have to start somewhere
Arduous, I say,
Calm and unique amid the obscurity
Of all things known
Almost a solemn space
From which we may contemplate
With ample gestures
The end of this autumn

Gradually, prudently, I go forward
With my notorious goosestep march

Through fields of wheat and fields of rye, and wild poppies –
Randomly strung years – or rather,
Time stretched out

Beyond its limits like an elongated piece of elastic –
While all else remained in place.
You could imagine the bracelet-watch
Turning into a clock
Or the Chinese peasant bent under his load
On a hot summer day
With his rice hat
And broken rickshaw abandoned
Right by the side of the Pink Panther
And that famous escapade of three squirrels
Out to gather nutmegs.
No one wanted to move a thing.
So many nights when you could have crept up
To the leafy realm of sound –
The drunken boat in the middle of the ocean,
You alone on the shore –
But oh no
You can't possibly hope for the showcase version of
the fate of young Robinson,
just imagine what it must be like after two days!
Sudden nightfall for Robinson,
When you no longer follow the rhythm of his breathing
In perfect harmony with his sleep
Like adjusting the radio
For the dull winter nights.
That child still full of joy and promises –
For children never put things off –
Alights on glow of ladybird and methods
To transform under the canopy of a symphonie fantastique.

Only then will you understand
How Ceasar's dwarf creeps up
The water pipes to greet Robinson
While Robinson himself
Is targeting the neighbouring flats

With his flamethrower

At the age of forty
Loneliness can be a treasure or a mental crisis
There you are, surrounded by your own food, own shit, own little poems,
And a layer of dirty humility will cover your body,
A package squeezed dry, not as a result of your choices
Or the years you've spent most inefficiently,
But simply the consequence
Of one indescribable performance.

I received a new pyjama
On the left breast pocket
'Obrega Hospital' is embroidered in red
This is where our new candy-coloured life starts
We're even allowed outside
Ghostly figures hunched
around two wooden stumps
We might even be allowed to fuck
Except they've stuffed us full of pills
To make us more spiritual
If I may say so
Can't afford to act like a madman
I wonder if Sartre scratched his head

I unwrapped the tinfoil
And wrapped it around the chicken thighs,

Thinking of an alternative –
Some icy octopus –
I waited till the thighs were cooked through
And the smell of onions, thyme and basil floated up.
I took the tray out, waited for it to cool down,
Went to unblock the toilet, humming some Dan Spataru song
'A pure-hearted man is waiting for you'

Even the worst junkie on this planet would have realised by now
Oh man, how lonely are you, oh man, do something,
Don't end up dying alone on that toilet, man!

15 lei scrounged off Tavi
And I'm able to regain my adolescent fervour
Interrupted now and then by plans for the future
Made with a courage I no longer have
Except when I was with Sonia,
When an aluminium spoon became
An American fighter plane
Bombing all and sundry.

There's no noble mystery haunting these hospital wards
No problems to scour our heads
Touch our limits
We are a problem of probability
We are here because we have problems
And were foolish enough to disclose that.

I waited for you Tuesday morning
I waited for you Tuesday lunchtime
I waited for you Tuesday evening
With a heart shrinking to the size of a flea
Or a pixel, rather

Translated by Marina Sofia

Miruna Vlada

*Nana

it wasn't late maybe around 9 at night
already dark
and i had already tucked myself in
and was waiting for her to come home
she had gone to a neighbor to ask for something
but it seemed like an eternity had passed
and she seemed not to be returning
i started trembling with fear under the blanket
panic rose with every minute that passed
my ears were ringing
what if she'll never come back to me?
she found me weeping
smelling her night gown
Nana was the only human
who took care of me
and for the few hours she was at the neighbor's house
i felt that without her
i had no one
every desertion lasts a lifetime
i wanted the smell of her body burned into my retina

Translated by Iarina Albu

The First Female Apostle.
Democracy Needs Your Body

it's certain – they don't wanna put their bodies on the line anymore!
they deny the social contract itself
that is holy in all democracies
supposedly they don't want to complicate their lives, sacrifice their careers or
simply don't want to give up the lifestyle they've gotten used to.
really? do you realize how far it's gone?
a democracy can't survive on air and a bunch of silly girls' whims
it needs new people
you'll see, we'll go back to a totalitarian regime soon
because of how feminism
brainwashed these new-generation women
democracy flows through their uterus
their weariness to make children will be our death you'll see

aaaaa, excuse me, mrs or miss?

Translated by Iarina Albu

*The Butterfly Effect

you're hearing the cranes' wing clapping
the gentle rustling from the storks' nests
hear only the shrieks
from the mating season of the rats
in the building's basement
i can feel them in the walls, the way they run full of desire
in every direction
but upstairs we're holding each other tightly in a nest
without letting even
one centimeter of unbreathed undistilled air
in between our temples

in your country the mango fruits are bursting now
just like the bronzed shoulders of
teenagers
and in ours rocks are bursting
between cranes bulldozers and stripped pipes
but a bit above them we're in each other
with deflowered lungs
with nails growing in each other
with our mango parfume
and loving irises

in your country it's the middle of the day now
scorching and good times
here it's night and rats started searching each other
and can't fit back
and our contorted bodies
leave no traces
just a howl
that smells of mango and loneliness

　　　***

there are only three types – unipear, multipear, nulipear.
in their medical files i'm a nulipear
that means i've never given birth.

my best friends are
the condom, the IUD, the contraceptive injections or
the surgical sterilization.

our grandmothers were the grand multipears – over 5 births
wow, so much flick-flack in only one generation!

we're the first women in Romania
that can have kids whenever we want.

we don't have to be a replica of what they want us to be
The Men in BOR[10]
The Men in The Romanian Academy
The Men who are CEOs
The Men at The National Bank
The Men at The Writers' Union
The Men Plastic Surgeons

it's cool being a nulipear
you don't worry and you have a lot of free time
but a higher risk of breast cancer
it's a barter
you win your freedom together with cervical cancer

Translated by Iarina Albu

---

[10] BOR is an abbreviation that stands for The Romanian Orthodox Church.

*Water is the Only Touch

she hasn't had sex in almost 3 years
when she misses it she gets in a full bath
and lets the water cling to her whole body
the water makes her feel less alone
she's 70% water and 30% loneliness now
she takes baths and goes swimming often
she puts on water she caresses herself with water she rubs herself against water
liquefied antidepressants sponsored by apanova and sometimes by
her overflowing lacrimal glands
she feels safe when water touches her skin
water doesn't ask her embarrassing questions
sometimes water sticks to her skin in beads. for a while it's good.
it almost never dries with towels
water tries to stay for a while on the skin
and then
it trickles it dries slowly it becomes unseen
she only feels alone when she has water beads on her this is
what it's come to.

Translated by Iarina Albu

Teona Galgoțiu

abrupt pleasure

i feel the abrupt pleasure when i get out of bed
and notice that the big tree in the garden penetrated the window
with a thick branch , it destroyed a lot around,
the light jumps on your changing face

another building close by has been demolished, I move quietly toward the mirror
look there's a robot making human mistakes
extracting pleasure from the asphalt's hardness into which it crashes
although it was programmed for something else

now we're on a train, the abrupt pleasure of the tracks jolts us
the mental torment incites us because it is the only infinite thing
we stretch our arms out the window and observe that
nothing saves us better than abrupt pleasure

the rhythmic walk of the people we see from the train
reminds me of the good decisions i sometimes took
the bad decision slowly approaches the bottom of the cold water,
which i visit in my memory

in my memory the cake is ready decorated with many candles and the sword with
    which we cut it every year,
and the illness with its beautiful crown sits in my memory on a throne,
and the sketch of the island awaits in my memory ,

over all these abrupt pleasure,
the only thing that guides me towards the world floats
like a dog with its leash full of saliva in its mouth

Translated by Andreea Iulia Scridon

treasure hunt

the wonderful strips around the city have grown shockingly fast
and those inside move back silently
the regression graduated and screwed onto trees replacing the plaques with Latin
    names
these transparent pills get lost on the transparent sidewalk
on which it is written don't look under me
watching, we notice the simple luminous point underneath us
which with a thought pushes us forcefully into the tight metallic strip
the name we're looking for is there but from the map just the corner

Translated by Andreea Iulia Scridon

fantastic fantasy

The fantasy of self-mutilation
blinks every evening in this semi-bourgeois animal with transparent skin
it stands in front of the mirror immobile
enough money for a nice bathroom
not enough to stop the bugs multiplying in the bag with seven types of seeds
or under the funnel used to fill bottles at the shiny water filter
from the mug bought in Vienna

the New Year's Eve party in Vienna took place a long time ago
there was nothing to do in the city
the layer of ice was beautiful only from a distance
same for the mirrors, all without exception,
from far away the image calms you
you see something recognizable no matter how weird as the name of the street
might sound
but every step closer
the fantasy cannot be ignored
and the street cracks with sound
you can see the fissure of the space

Translated by Andreea Iulia Scridon

Lena Chilari

today i found out that my poetry manuscript is going to be published

yet i've never been more miserable
crying&lonely&helpless
because i don't make a cent writing
and don't bring honor to my family by getting married
i'm 25 years old and i still live with my parents
because i haven't saved enough money to move out alone
i haven't made any difference in this world
and i laugh and cry as if it were the last time
i called the boy i love and he rejected me
should i thank him for making me write a semester ago
i cursed myself for writing about myself and not about
violence&homosexuality&corruptions&the sick society from which I hail
i received three roses from a boy i don't know
and i cried in front of my little icon because i didn't kill myself today either
i kissed the father who raised me and
listened to the sighs of my mother for whom i am a disappointment
i have ambition&energy&resolve&love&care
i offer what i lack
and i can't stop writing or crying
today i found out that my pathetic poetry manuscript is going to be published
in an email that got my last name wrong
and for whom i don't matter in any way
hello to more people who won't understand me
hello to more people for whom i'll remain an absolute nobody
hello to those who consider me hysterical&suicidal&unfit for letters
instead of becoming a voice or a much desired change
or at least a daughter worthy of pride

Translated by Andreea Iulia Scridon

i scald my lips with coffee and lie down on my belly

in order to look into the eyes of little helena in which i see myself.
she's two years old and wants crêpes without
sugar because sugar is forbidden
you can die from it as you can die from
"жыве́ Белару́сь!"
i look at her and realize
that she will not be beaten with a belt or verbally abused
and left without food as punishment
like masha from russia or aliona from the village of pepeni
she will not be hunted and shot in the woods of moldova
accused of not wearing the right clothes or of raising her tail
raped and victimized by all goods
she will not be kidnapped like kolesnikova
in the middle of the street by pro-clown mustachios
or poisoned like navalny by pro-putiners
innocent children born of ignorant idiots
become depressed
and commit suicide
and instead of talking about everyone's personal choice
about happiness mental health
loneliness or about the right partners for us
we wonder when we should get married and pop out brats
"it's time to have your own"
to bring you a cup of novichok in your old age
do not dare to avoid suffering and die quickly
i swallow hard and grab helena by the hand
she is not my child nor will she be anytime soon
— i pour coffee down my throat
— i bite into the pancake with extra chocolate
more than the novichok navalny was able drink from his tea at tomsk
and i slowly salvage myself from all the days left to me
in a world as wonderful
and as fertile as ours

Translated by Andreea Iulia Scridon

cracking the mirror with my fist i noticed

how little helena nestles in my eyes
with her golden eyes in which i see
mom at the kitchen window with her cup
drinking coffee
"life is so beautiful, mother" says the good man
not helena's mother
i see my goliath stupider than
the earth can bear and i splash juice on him
i see myself kicked out of the house at night
in the green satin dress
with a broken and rotten heart where i
wanted to take my eyes out my skull and
cut my ears off from the flesh to neither see nor hear
that i am not wanted or loved or welcomed
— postmodern oedipus the pale wo man
with holes in my palms that can't cry
log out • lena • jump • put on the package of
plastic • swallow the bottle or pill • strangle yourself
damn you —live but don't become like them
you're supposed to use writing as a medium
confront reality • black lives matter • all lives matter
but does my own life matter?
that is the question, helena, that's what you will experience until
you won't take anymore
your golden eyes out of your skull
little by little

Translated by Andreea Iulia Scridon

alphabet

i wasn't careful when they changed the key to the front door
my parents pour their venom into foreign lands
and i study letters and can't even succeed in typing into them
a absence of the mother
b bucks
c chilari
d damn why the hell am I here
e elena after grandma
f for my brother
g grigore
h hunger
i "isn't she intellijent"
î is on loan from i
j jabbing jaded
k 600 km away
l ludmila is
m my mother
n the name of my bulgarian people
o oh i'm a disappointment anyway
p for her paradise
q
r
s
tata, i love you
this is as far as i could get for the two of you

Translated by Andreea Iulia Scridon

poem ∞

when i was little
i was born strangled
with the maternal umbilical cord around my neck
when i grew older
i choked on my own flesh
on sharp fingers
when i was little
i asked my mother for love
and she turned her back on me and i cried
when i grew older
i thought for a long time that this was the definition of love
and i failed
when i was little
I saw the earth shake under my father's laughter
when i was big
i understood that my father was nothing more than the core of the earth
when i was small
i wanted to be thin and to have long hair
when i grew older
i became so beautiful in my soul
that it flows over my eternally short hair
and it doesn't even matter anymore how i look
my poetry is not beautiful words and rhymes
my poetry is feeling then pain then ink then keyboard then agony then pleasure
and finally healing
i carry the stigma of weak love in the cracks of my soles
as i straighten my back and raise my head towards the sun
small or big
lenuța or elena
six or twenty-six
chilàri or chìlari —
a turned back does not define me
and the earth cracks under my soles blessed with bunions
there is no person in this world happier than me

Translated by Andreea Iulia Scridon

you suck on my breast, achilles,

and venom flows from the corner of your smile
the statue of a woman,
laughs the tour guide, is the statue of a prostitute
— every free and beautiful woman is a prostitute —
depth seems transparent with you
you break limits open, my love,
and your stinging kiss leaves sand between my teeth
youth does not make you poison yourself
you milk me, and i swell like a pregnant cow
i don't know what it is you're trying to squeeze out of me:
love passion sensuality madness
you are naive and believe in the future
do you think i'll come back to you tomorrow
do you think that your father will like you and who knows:
you won't be like him
— we are us but we are ours, this i strongly believe —
little helena's eyes are full of the violence in belarus
she has turned one year old and greedily collects cones
she puts them in her father's brown pants
like grenades in the pants of belarusian civilians
you enter me, achilles,
like bayonets of OMONs into the bottoms of belarusian civilians
lukashenko has a musty milk mustache
and ceaușescu seems to be resurrected from worm-ridden mulch
— my love, i know you could do immoral things if need be —
you were told that in the chest there is a heart in the shape of a bent-over ass
inside me there is a rust-tinted missing phallic rib
you look at me but my gaze is an abyss
which doesn't look back at you
enter me, my love,
but don't make me forget what's going on in the world
—or we weren't born in the right countries to truly love each other

Translated by Andreea Iulia Scridon

when i was punched

in pavilion 21, psychiatry department
i prayed to the ceiling
let my father come and save me
i promised i would believe in gods
that i would sacrifice my wrists
and dirty ankles
i would do my own injections to
numb my senses
and i went to the bathroom
i gave birth to a baby whose name
i don't remember anymore
i wanted to make up a story of creation for him
worthy of novels
but the door closed and i remained in the pavilion
the section door is a heavy door
i can barely open it
it can hardly be opened by anyone outside
when i didn't know how to eat
i ate my family
and i refused to go to the bathroom ever again
i wanted them to stay with me forever
my belly swelled and my veins cracked
i then drilled my eyes out and said to myself
now is the time to go blind
maybe they'll move me to another pavilion
to another section
i continued to eat whatever i could find
doctors friends come to visit buddies passersby strangers
i never got my fill
pavilion 21, the psychiatric ward was in me
i wanted to be loved and kissed
but who can kiss a feminist
a feminist in the pavilion is a new public target

for stones

i shot myself

i said I was going to die by my own hand

so huge so irrational so alone

the pavilion swallowed me even though i was bigger than it was

now, that i have no escape

tell me ceiling

can i repent of everything i believed in with all my might when i was

at home with my father

Translated by Andreea Iulia Scridon

i have known only one night of love

in which the field of fire turned into lava
the earth flowed
i too flowed with it
the plains moaned
my partner moaned too
he swallowed my fingers like pasta
my hair dripped into every hidden hole
i watched everything that was happening clearly
i told myself softly
so this is what i was made for
my partner's skull cracked open with pleasure
i knew that eternity was inside me
and that no one has access to it

Translated by Andreea Iulia Scridon

holding your urine in while looking at a screen is a common thing to do

the image fades when a child warns you
my pain hurts
and all you can do is pull your hair out
strand by strand
and pass them between your lips
as if you weren't breastfed enough
or not breastfed at all
it's a Freudian game
we talk all the time about discrimination
gender equality
and you draw imaginary lines with your finger on the top of your head
this is where all the world's discrimination will fall
at a job where you are humiliated
and poorly paid
where at the end of the day
romania has not been gentle with those like you
it puts you in a national railway train compartment
with an orthodox priest who wants to massage you
at midnight
he stinks like a pig little girl
what do you want to be good to everyone
the light fades the door stays
open
between being raped or robbed
said the poet
i prefer my mother who beats me at home
in front of a mirror kissed with cheap
lipstick from the market

Translated by Andreea Iulia Scridon

dad, i drank four glasses of wine yesterday and vomited

real good, three glasses and some cause i spilled one
i had a poetry reading in which i stammered and
you know how important it is to me
not to stammer
i had a reading in which i cried over a poem
about you and you know how important it is to me
to cry
dad, now that i'm 26 and doing what i love
you say to get my life together
we're in the hospital
you look at me and ask me about money
and i look away
dad, i cried so hard
the entire city of Brașov resounded
i cried so much that i
wanted to die immediately
to stop the pain
dad, i can't tell you anything
it would only hurt you and they've only just
taken out your first kidney
dad, you don't understand that i am
a sad adult and that money doesn't matter yet
i am writing this poem in the book i gave
you and then took it back
i took everything from you, dad
and you always ask me if I want more
when you die you will not be buried with
my book in your hand
but with my tears all fallen into the emptiness

Translated by Andreea Iulia Scridon

The Poets

TEODORA COMAN (b.1976) poet and editor of Poesis International. She has published five poetry collections: *cârtița de mansardă (the attic mole)* (2012), *foloase necuvenite (illicit gains)* (2017), *soft guerrilla* (2019), *Lucy* (2021) *Piesă de rezistență (Piece of resistence)*, (2023).

DAN DEDIU (b. 1986) published the volume of poetry *4.5 litri de sânge, miliardar(4.5 liters of blood, billlionaire)* (2017).

ANDRA ROTARU (b. 1980) is the author of *Într-un pat sub cearșaful alb (In a bed under the white sheet)* (2005), *Ținuturile sudului (Southern territories)(*2010), *Lemur* (2012) and *Tribar* (2018). She was awarded The Best Young Poet of Year Award at The Writers' Gala in Bucharest (2013) for *Lemur*. Currently she is writer in residence of the city of Graz, Austria.

MIHÓK TAMÁS (b. 1991) is a bilingual poet, translator and book editor and deputy editor of the cultural magazine "Familia". He graduated from the Philology Department of University of Oradea. Author of five poetry books in Romanian: *Șantier în rai (Construction site in heaven)(*2013), *winrar de tot(totally winrar)* (2015), *cuticular* (2017), *biocharia. ritual ecolatru(biocharia.ecolatric ritual)* (2020) and *æs alienum* (2024) and of two poetry books in Hungarian: *cuticulum vitae* (2017) and *rizómazaj* (2021). He has translated poetry books written by Radu Vancu, Constantin Virgil Bănescu, Krusovszky Dénes and Balázs F. Attila, an anthology of contemporary Romanian poets and an anthology of contemporary Hungarian poets. He is co-founder of „Pragul Vaida", the main reading club from his hometown, Oradea.

MUGUR GROSU (b.1973) writer, visual artist & journalist. He is the author of 6 poetry books: *Haltera cu zurgălăi* (2001); *sms / ei respiră și fac dragoste ca și fluturii (sms/they breathe and make love like butterflies)* (2006), *troleul 43 s-a spânzurat cu cordonul de la capot (the tolleybus 43 hanged itself with the robe cord* (2009*), Grossomodo* (2011), *principala morengo* (2021) and *vedere din uman* (2024) and two prose volumes *Măcelărie (Butcher shop)*(2006) and *Status* (2013).

DAN COMAN (b. 1975) writes poetry and prose. He is the author of four poetry books *anul cârtiței galbene* (*the year of the yellow mole*) (2003), *ghinga* (2005), *Dicționarul Mara (Mara dictionary)* (2009) and *Insectarul Coman (Coman insectarium)* *(*2017) and six fiction books: *Irezistibil* (*Irresistible)* (2010), *Parohia (The Parish)* (2012, 2017), *Căsnicie (Marriage)* (2015, 2016), *aceste lucruri care nu se vor schimba niciodată (these things will never change)* (2019), *Ce preferi? (What would you like?)* (2022). He organizes the Bistrița International Festival of Poetry and Music.

FLORIN PARTENE (b. 1974). He published: *Reverența (Reverence)* (2007, 2009), *Liber de causis* (2013), *Poeme pentru începători(Poems for beginners)* (2023). He is present with poems in several magazines and anthologies.

LIVIA ȘTEFAN (b. 1982) is a poet, translator and performer. She published the poetry volumes *re.volver* (2012), *Lolita32* (2016) and *Thanato Hotel* (2019).

DOMNICA DRUMEA (b. 1979) is a poet and translator. She is a founding member of the first important post-2000 literary movement in Romania, *Fracturi (Fractures)*. She debuted in 2004 with the volume *Crize (Crises)*. In 2009, she published the volume *Not for Sale,* and in 2014 he published the volume *Vocea (The voice)*. She has translated several books of contemporary literature from English.

DIANA GEACĂR (b. 1984) is a poet, prose writer and translator from the English language. She has published the volumes of good poetry, *bună, eu sunt diana și sunt colega ta de cameră (hi, my name is diana and I am your roommate)* (2005), *Frumusețea bărbatului căsătorit (The beauty of the married man)* ((2009) and *Dar noi suntem oameni obișnuiți (But we are ordinary people)* (2017), children books and the volume of short prose *Cine locuiește la subsol* (*Who lives in the basement)* (2018).

LIGIA KEŞIŞIAN (b. 1988) is a poet, translator, DJ and festival curator. She has published the poetry volumes *Mici cutremure (small earthquakes)* (2017), *Miss Houdini* (2019) and *Anul tigrului de apă (The year of the water tiger)* (2023).

DUMITRU FANFAROV (b. 1993) is a poet, rapper and MC, the author of the volume *of steppe and trance poetry* (2020) and several albums, under the label *Peace the gun.*

TEODOR DUNĂ (b. 1981). He graduated from the Faculty of Letters, University of Bucharest. He has published the volumes: *trenul de troieşunu februarie (the train of february thirt first)* (2002), *catafazii (cataphasia)* (2005), *de-a viul(playing alive),* (2010), *obiecte umane (human objects),* (2015), *kirilă* (2017) and *flaşneta babel (the babel hurdy-gurdy)* (2022). In 2019, *Minunata lume (Wonderful world),* an anthology of his poems was published by Cartier Publishing House.

CĂTĂLINA STANISLAV (b. 1995) is a poet and a translator. She graduated from the Faculty of Letters in Sibiu in 2017 and has a Master's degree in Romanian Language and Literature from the same faculty. She holds an MA in Gender Studies from Utrecht University (The Netherlands). She is co-editor of Z9 Magazine and co-organizer of the Z9 International Poetry Festival, now in its 9th edition. *Nu mă întrerupe (Don't interupt me)* is her debut poetry book published in 2021.

ANA DONŢU (b. 1985) published the volume of poetry *Cadrul 25 (Frame 25)* (2015) and the volume of short stories *Varşava (Warsawa)* (2019).

ROBERT GABRIEL ELEKES (b. 1985) is a Germanist and teaches at "Transilvania" University in Braşov. He has published the volumes of poetry *Aici îmi iau dinţii-n spinare şi adio (Here I carry my teeth on my back and say good bye)* (2015) and *o dronă care să mă vrea în sfârşit doar pe mine (finally a drone that wants only me)* (2018).

ANASTASIA GAVRILOVICI (b. 1995) debuted with the volume of poetry *Industria liniştirii adulţilor (The adults pacification industry) (*2019) and has translated books by Kurt Vonnegut and Ernesto Cardenal, currently working on translating a massive anthology of Louise Glück's poetry.

ANDREI DÓSA (b. 1985) has published three novels and the volumes of poetry *Când va veni ceea ce este desăvârșit (When that which is perfect will come)* (2011), *American Experience* (2013), *Nada* (2015), *adevăratul băiat de aur (the true golden boy)* (2017), *Expectativa Luminoasă (The Bright Expectation)* (2020) and *Ultima familie tradițională (The last traditional family)* (2024). He translated into Romanian several novels and volumes of important Hungarian writers and an anthology of young Hungarian poets from Transylvania.

CLAUDIU KOMARTIN (b. 1983) published *Păpușarul și alte insomnii (The Puppeteer and Other Insomnia)* (2003), *Circul domestic (Domestic Circus)* (2005), *Un sezon în Berceni (A Season in Berceni)* (2009), *Cobalt* (2013), *Maeștrii unei arte muribunde (Masters of a Dying Art)* (2010-2017) (2017), *Autoportet în flacăra de sudură (Self-Portrait in the Welding Flame)* (2021), *17 poeme de dragoste si un pantoum imperfect (17 Love Poems and an Imperfect Pantoum)* (2022) and *Inoculare (Inoculation)* (2022). He is also a translator, editor and anthologist.

MERLICH SAIA (b. 1982) is the literary pseudonym of Eugen Vuțescu, a Romanian medical doctor, poet, and visual artist. His debut volume, *Garda de Corp (The Bodyguard)*, published in 2014 won some of the most prestigious Romanian literary prizes. His second volume *Cutia toracică (The Rib Cage)* was published in 2022. As a visual artist, Eugen Vuțescu works in a variety of mediums: photography, painting, and installation art.

OLGA ȘTEFAN (b. 1988) is a poet and teacher, with a doctorate in Philology. She has published the volumes of poetry: *Toate ceasurile (All the clocks)* (2006), *Saturn, zeul (Saturn, the god)* (2016), *Charles Dickens* (2017), *Civilizații (Civilisations)*(2020), *Resursa (The resource)* (2022) and *Bestia de zahăr (The sugar beast)* (2024).

MINA DECU (b. 1983), poet, translator and creative writing teacher. In 2018 she published *Desprindere (Detachment)* that received numerous prizes and, in 2024, *Tagliatelle allegro* translated in English by Anca Roncea și Rajnesh Chakrapani.

RADU NIȚESCU (b. 1992) has published the poetry volumes *gringo* (2012), *Dialectica urșilor (The dialectic of bears)*(2016) and *Satao* (2020) and translated poetry from English (Kenneth Rexroth, Kenneth Koch, Mark Strand).

VLAD DIMITRIU writes poetry. His volume *Yetica & Barbital* was published by frACTalia Publishing House in 2018.

CRISTINA ISPAS (b. 1979) published the poetry volumes *fetița. vinyl mix (the girl. vinyl mix)* (2007), *rezervația (the reservation)* (2011) and *40. să înceapă jocurile (40. let the games begin)* (2018). Together with V. Leac, she coordinated the thematic anthology *Generația de aur (The golden generation)* (2020).

RADU VANCU (b. 1978) is a Romanian poet, novelist, scholar, and translator. Between 2019 and 2023, he has served as president of PEN Romania. He is a professor at the Faculty of Letters and Arts at the „Lucian Blaga" University in Sibiu. He is editor-in-chief of the Transilvania magazine, as well as an editor of the Poesis Internațional magazine. Since 2002, he published nine volumes of poetry, for which he was awarded several national and international prizes; his poetry has been translated into 20 languages, either in anthologies/magazines or as individual books. He has also published a novel, Transparența (2018), and two volumes of a diary (2017, 2021), which were awarded several prizes. He is the president of the International Poetry Festival in Sibiu Poets in Transylvania.

DAN SOCIU (b. 1978) is a writer, editor and translator. He studied political science, philosophy and Romanian and Slavonic studies at the Alexandru Ioan Cuza University in Iasi. He is considered one of the representative poets of the „miserabilist" generation. In 2006, his work *cântece eXcesive (eXcessive songs)* was awarded *Best Book of the Year* by the Romanian Writers' Association. He published eight volumes of poetry *borcane bine legate, bani pentru încă o săptămână (tightly tied jars, money for another week)* (2002), *fratele păduche (brother louse)* (2004), *cântece eXcesive (eXcessive songs)* (2005), *Pavor nocturn* (2011), *Poezii naive și sentimentale (Naive and sentimental poems)* (2012), *Vino cu mine știu exact unde mergem (come with me i know exactly where we're going)* (2013), *Uau! (Wow!)* (2019), *17 poezii (17 poems)* (2021), and three novels *Urbancolia (Urbancholia)* (2008), *Nevoi speciale (Special needs)* (2008), *Combinația (The combination)* (2012). He translated and published selections from the poetry of Charles Bukowski and Seamus Heaney.

MEDEEA IANCU is a poet and director, the author of several volumes of poems, among which: *Delacroix este tabu: Suita romînească (Delacrox is taboo: The Romanian Suite* (2017), *Delacrox is taboo: The lyrical amendments* (2019), *Țesătoarea. Opera instrumentală (The weaver. Instrumental work)* (2023). She coordinated the *Arta revendicării. Antologie de poezie feministă (The Art of Claiming. An anthology of feminsit poetry)* (2020).

RĂZVAN ȚUPA (b.1975) studied History of Religions and Culture and works as a journalist. His books include *Fetiș (Fetish)* (2001), *corpuri românești(romanian bodies)* (2005), *poetic. cerul din delft și alte corpuri românești(poetic.the sky in delft and other romanian bodies)* (2011), *poetic. relația grafică (poetic. the graphic relation)* (2022) *poetic.interfața sonoră (poetic. sound interface)* (2022). An anthology of his poems, *poetic relațional (poetic relational)* was published by Cartier Publishing House in Chishinev in 2024. He devised *Poeticile cotianului (The poetics of the everyday)*, a series of weekly literary meetings that went on for five years (145 meetings). *Poeticile cotidianului – de la seri de literatură în mișcare la Republica Poetica (The poetics of the everyday — from evenings of literature in motion to Republica Poetica),* a book where the evenings of literature he organised between 2005 and 2010 are documented was published in 2015.

V. LEAC (b. 1973) is a poet and a visual artist. He has published several books of poetry, most of them in several revised editions: *Seymour: sonata pentru cornet de hârtie (Seymour: sonata for paper cornet)* (2005, 2006, 2013), *Dicționar de vise (Dreams dictionary)* (2006), *Lucian – un experiment (Lucian-an experiment)* (2009), *Toți sunt îngrijorați (Everyone is worried)* (2010, 2015) *Unchiul este încântat (Uncle is delighted)* (2013), *Monoideal* (2018). Founding member of the literary group *Celebrul animal* and of the *Ca și Cum (As If)* magazine. In 2012, together with Bianca Băilă, he founded MOI in Timișoara; curator of the event W.A.D. Arad, 2014. Experimental movies: *The Village Drones* (I) (2014), *The Village Drones* (II) (2015) and *Trasee descriptive cu intrus (Descriptive Trajectories with Intruder)*, (2016), *Chat la Moinești (Chat at Moinești)* (2017). Editor of the poetry anthology *Perturbări în desfășurare. O antologie a prezentului (Disturbances in progress. An anthology of the present)* (2021).

TIBERIU NEACŞU (b. 1981) is a poet and translator. He graduated from the Faculty of Letters in Craiova. He debuted in 2000 with the volume *Nebuna*. His second book of poetry, *Acrobat în zece pași (Acrobat in ten steps)*, was published in 2013. He translated from Amiri Baraka, Peg Boyers, Lloyd Schwartz, Derek JG Williams, Ani Gjika, Mustafa Köz, W.H. Auden, Anne Carson, etc. and is the anthologist and translator of the volume *Miile de tehnologii ale extazului (The thousands technologies of ecstasy)*, poems by Frank Bidart. He is co-founder of the Matca Cenacle.

RITA CHIRIAN (b. 1982) holds a doctorate in Letters, with the thesis *Sandalele lui Empedocle. Anatomia mutațiilor po(i)etice postcomuniste (Empedocles' sandals. Anatomy of post-communist po(i)ethical mutations)* (2012), she writes chronicle and essay and has translated books from French and English. She published the volumes of poetry: *Sevraj (Withdrawal)* (2006), *poker face* (2010), *Asperger* (2012), *Casa fleacurilor (The house of trifles)* (2016) and *Medusa* (2024).

ELENA VLĂDĂREANU (b. 1981) debuted with the experimental autofiction volume *pagini (pages)* (2002), followed by the poetry volumes *Fisuri (Cracks)* (2003), *Europa. Zece cântece funerare (Europe. Ten funeral songs)* (2005), *Spațiu privat (Private space)* (2009), *Non Stress Test* (2016), *Bani. Muncă. Timp liber (Money. Work. Free Time)* (2017), *Minunata lume Disney (The wonderful Disney World)* (2019), the anthology *Ce pot distinge în întunericul sălii. Poeme alese 2002-2020 (What can I make out in the darkness of the room. Selected poems)* (2022) and by *Teatru intim (Intimate theater)* (2018, together with Robert Bălan).

RUXANDRA NOVAC (b. 1980). Considered today one of the spearheads of the *Fracturi (Fractures)* group, which dominated the literary production of the beginning of the millennium, Ruxandra Novac began writing poetry during high school. She is the author of the volumes *ecograffiti. poeme pedagogice. steaguri pe turnuri (ecograffiti. pedagogical poems. flags on towers* (2003, 2005, 2018) and *Alwarda* (2020).

ADRIAN DINIȘ (1986-2018) was born and lived in Bucharest, where he graduated from the Romanian-American University. He published *Poezii Odioase de Dragoste (Odious Love Poems)* (2010) and then delayed publishing his second book. *Toate zborurile au fost anulate (All flights have been cancelled)* contains most of the poems written in the last years of his life and a selection from his first volume.

VERONICA ȘTEFĂNEȚ (b. 1985) published the volume of poetry *Scrum (Ash)* (2019) and co-translated into Romanian, together with Victor Țvetov, an anthology of contemporary Russian poetry, *Tot ce poți cuprinde cu vederea (Everything you can see)* (2019).

ALEX VĂSIEȘ (b. 1993) is a poet, editor and translator (Chuck Palahniuk, Graeme Macrae Burnet, Tom Hanks), author of the poetry volumes *lovitura de cap (the head short)* (2012), *Oana Văsieș* (2016) and *Instalația (The Installation)* (2016).

GABI EFTIMIE (b. 1981), who has also writes as "greenplastic," debuted in 2006 with the volume *ochi roșii polaroid / acesta este un test* (*polaroid red eyes / this is a test*), which earned her the România Literară debut award. It was followed in 2014 by *Nordul e o stare de spirit (The North is a state of mind)* and more recently by *Sputnik in grădină (Sputnik in the garden)* (2020).

RĂZVAN ANDREI (b. 1981) is a poet, translator and editor, the author of the poetry volumes *Jazz pentru iguane (Jazz for Iguanas)* (2018) and *Raport către Walt Whitman (Report to Walt Whitman)*(2022). He is working on a new translation of Walt Whitman's poetry.

ȘTEFAN MANASIA (b. 1977). He is a poet and journalist, editor of the culture magazine Tribuna. In 2008, he initiated, in Cluj, the "Nepotu lui Thoreau" Reading Club (along with Szántai János and François Bréda) — the most important Romanian-Hungarian literary community in Transylvania. He published six volumes of poems: *Amazon și alte poeme (Amazon and other poems)(2003)*, *cartea micilor invazii (the book of small invasions)* (2008), *bicicleta de lemn (the wooden bycicle)* (2011), *Bonobo sau cucerirea spațiului (Bonobo or the conquest of space)* (2013), *Cerul senin (Clear sky)* (2015), *Gustul cireșelor (The taste of cherries)* (2017), *Cronovizorul (The chronovisor)* (2020), *Platanii din Samothraki (The plane trees of Samothraki)* (2022), *Etica grunge. Sîntem generația extincției (The Ethic of Grunge. We are the extinction generation)* (2023) and *Sursele obscure (Obscure sources)* (2024). He is the author of the volume of essays and literary chronicles *Stabilizator de aromă (Aroma stabilizer)* (2016). He summarizes his (meta)poetic credo as: "Man, this mystic bug." (Summa Theologica).

MIRCEA ANDREI FLOREA (b. 1996) is a mathematician and poet, the author of the volumes *Larvae (Larvae)* (2020) and *Grija (Care)* (2023).

GEORGE VASILIEVICI (1978-2010) published the volumes of poetry *Gabi78* (2001), *Featuring* (2004), together with Ștefan Caraman and Ondine Dietz), *Cerneală (Ink)* (2004), *O cameră cu două camere (A room with two rooms)* (2006), *WC-rul* (2007) and two novels, *Yoyo* (2008) and *Viseptol* (published posthumously in 2011), and his work was collected in 2020 in the book *Antologia George Vasilievici (The George Vasilievici Anthology)*.

CRISTINA STANCU (b. 1990) made her poetry debut with *teritorii (territories)* in 2017, a collection that earned her both the National Debut Poetry Prize "Mihai Eminescu" and the National Debut Poetry Prize "Iustin Panța." In 2021, she published her second book, *apără pe cineva de tine (protect someone from you)*, a work that explores how we internalize the constant flow of information from both the digital and analog worlds. Her poetry takes on an experimental edge, questioning reality itself.

IULIA MILITARU is a writer and editor at frACTalia Press, and part of the Literature and Feminism and Cooperativa Arbore collectives. She has published several volumes of experimental literature and critical theory, including: *Confiscarea bestiei. O postcercetare* (*Seizing the beast. A post-research*) (2016), *Atlas (auto)mat/on (auto)BIO/graphy/I© de câteva tipuri principale de discursuri* (*Atlas (auto)mat/on (auto)BIO/graphy/I© of several main types of discourses*) (2017: in electronic version, reedited 2019: in print version), *Metaforic și metonimic: o tipologie a poeziei* (*Metaphorical and metonymic: a typology of poetry*) (2011), *Literature and the phenomenon of alienation* (vol. I, 2020). As early as 2018, she started working on the Maia Șerbănescu project, to imagine new forms of material existence, alternative sexualities and bodily transformations through the permanent reconfiguration of social relations in different environments. She has become a hybrid entity, author of the volumes: *Fuck off, Mr. Charcot!* (2019) and *OikosLogia. Știința casei socialiste și a ființelor posibile* (*Oikoslogia. The science of the socialist home and possible beings*) (2022).

MONICA STOICA (b.1990) graduated from the Faculty of Letters, department of Universal and Comparative Literature at the University of Bucharest. She also graduated in Theater Direction at UNATC Bucharest. She was a journalist at Infinitezimal, Mediafax, Jurnalul and Hotnews/Perspektiva. Her first volume, *fetele visează electric (the girls dream electric)* was published in 2019. Her second volume, *pop surreal land*, was publihed in 2014.

FLORENTIN POPA (b. 1989) is a poet and ambient electronic / spoken word performer. He published the poetry volumes *Trips, heroes & love songs* (2013), *Efrafa* (2017), *Dezintegrare(Disintegration)* (2021) and *Sutta* (2024).

T. S . KHASIS (1975-2025) In 2005 he published *Arta scalpării (The art of scalping)*. He further published three more volumes *pe datorie (on debt)* (2011), *aparenta naturalețe a vieții (the apparent naturalness of life)* (2015) and *Plăcerea spectacolului (The pleasure of the show)* (2023).

MIRUNA VLADA (b. 1986) is a poet and professor of political science and has published the poetry volumes *Poeme extrauterine (Extrauterine poems)* (2004), *Pauza dintre vene (The pause between the veins)* (2007), *Bosnia. Partaj (Bosnia. Divorce sharing)* (2014) and *Premature (Premature)* (2021).

TEONA GALGOȚIU (b. 1998) is a writer and a filmmaker. She founded the "Gura Mare" platform, which explores poetry through interdisciplinary projects, for which she received the "Gheorghe Iova" poetic experiment award. In 2020 she debuted with the poetry book *I look back and it's gone* at OMG Publishing ("Iustin Panța" debut prize, ARCCA Poetry book of the year). In 2025 her play *Memories of snow* will have its premiere at the theatre of Essen, in Germany.

LENA CHILARI (b. 1995) graduated from the Cluj Faculty of Letters. She is a poet, performer and organizer of spoken word events. She published the volumes *o cană de noviciok la bătrânețe* (*a cup of noviciok in old age*) (2020) and *Liudmila răstoarnă munții (Liudmila topples mountains)* (2024).

The Translators

ANDREEA SCRIDON is a translator and poet. Born in Romania, she immigrated with her parents to the United States as a child and grew up in Florida. She studied Comparative Literature at King's College London and Creative Writing at the University of Oxford. As a hybrid of two cultures, she has translated extensively from Romanian into English and she is acknowledged as one of the most prolific translators of contemporary Romanian poetry.

MARINA SOFIA is a translator (from Romanian and German into English), reviewer, editor and writer of mainly poetry and flash fiction. She is the co-founder of Corylus Books, publishing crime fiction in translation. She is also a global nomad, which sounds much better than immigrant. Her translations have been highly commended by Modern Poetry in Translation, the John Dryden Translation Prize and the Stephen Spender trust.

ALINA ŞTEFĂNESCU is a writer, editor and translator. Recent books include a creative nonfiction chapbook, *Ribald* (Bull City Press Inch Series, Nov. 2020) and *Dor*, which won the Wandering Aengus Press Prize (September, 2021). Her debut fiction collection, Every Mask I Tried On, won the Brighthorse Books Prize (April 2018). Alina's poems, essays, and fiction can be found in Prairie Schooner, North American Review, World Literature Today, Pleiades, Poetry, BOMB, Crab Creek Review, and others. She serves as editor, reviewer, and critic for various journals and is currently working on a novel-like creature. Her new poetry collection will be published by Sarabande in 2025. More online at www.alinastefanescuwriter.com.

IARINA ALBU followed a Bachelor's in Russian and French Language and Literature in Cluj-Napoca and is currently pursuing a Master's in Linguistics in Utrecht. She has contributed to translation projects before in both prose and non-fiction, but this marks her debut venture into the art of translating poetry.

CLAUDIA SEREA is a Pushcart Prize winning poet and translator. She has published seven poetry collections, most recently *In Those Years, No One Slept* (Broadstone Books, 2023). Serea is a founding editor of National Translation Month, and she co-edited and co-translated *The Vanishing Point That Whistles*, an Anthology of Contemporary Romanian Poetry (Talisman House Publishing, 2011). She also translated from Romanian Adina Dabija's *Beautybeast* (Northshore Press, 2012) and Iulia Militaru's *The Seizure of the Beast. A Post-research* (Guernica Editions, 2023). Serea serves on the board of The Red Wheelbarrow Poets and is one of the curators of the Red Wheelbarrow Poetry Readings. She writes, translates, and edits manuscripts in Rutherford, New Jersey.

CLARA BURGHELEA published two poetry collections: *The Flavor of the Other* (Dos Madres Press 2020) and *Praise the Unburied* (Chaffinch Press 2021). Her poems and translations have been published in Goalf Coast, Delos, The Los Angeles Review and elsewhere. She is the Review Editor of Ezra, An Online Journal of Translation.

ANCA RONCEA is a graduate of the Iowa Writers' Workshop, University of Iowa's MFA in Literary Translation and is currently a PhD student in Comparative Literature (International Writers' Track) at Washington University in Saint Louis. Anca's poetry has been published in the Berkeley Poetry Review, Beecher's Magazine, Omniverse, the Bare Life Review, and Lana Turner. Her translation from Romanian of the poetry collection *Tribar* by Andra Rotaru was published in 2022 by Saturnalia. She is currently working on her first book of poetry, an experimental translation that creates a speculative archive of the work and presence of women artists of the Dada Movement.

CĂTĂLINA STANISLAV is a poet and translator. She graduated from the Faculty of Letters in Sibiu in 2017 and has a Master's degree in Romanian Language and Literature from the same faculty. She holds an MA in Gender Studies from Utrecht University (The Netherlands). She is co-editor of Z9 Magazine and co-organizer of the Z9 International Poetry Festival, now in its 9th edition. *Nu mă întrerupe (Don't interupt me)* is her debut poetry book published in 2021.

ALEX VĂSIEȘ is a poet, editor and translator (Chuck Palahniuk, Graeme Macrae Burnet, Tom Hanks), the author of the poetry volumes *Headbutt* (2012), *Oana Văsieș* (2016) and *Instalația* (2016).

ANDREW DAVIDSON-NOVOSIVSCHEI is a teacher, poet and translator from Arizona, settled in Bucharest since 2015. He writes poetry in Romanian and English and has published in Poesis International, Tribuna, Apricity Press, Poetic Stand, etc. The poem *the taste of freedom* was nominated for the US Pushcart Prize. In 2022 he exhibited a solo "pop-up book" show with illustrated lyrics at Diptych Art Space. He has been invited to festivals such as Poezia e la Bistrița (Poetry is in Bistrița) , the Bucharest International Poetry Festival, the Iași International Literature and Translation Festival (FILIT), and to reading clubs such as Cenaclul Republica and the Max Blecher Institute. His literary translations have been published in magazines such as Asymptote Journal, Trafika Europe, Šamd, and won scholarships from the Romanian Cultural Institute and FILIT.

The Editors

PAUL DORU MUGUR is a writer, translator and editor. He co-edited and co-translated four poetry anthologies as follows: *Born in Utopia, an Anthology of Modern and Contemporary Romanian Poetry* (Talisman House Publishing, 2006), *The Vanishing Point That Whistles, an Anthology of Contemporary Romanian Poetry* (Talisman House Publishing, 2011), *Locul Nimănui, O Antologie de Poezie Contemporană Americană* (*No One's Place. An Anthology of Contemporary American Poetry*), (Cartea Românească, București, 2006) translated from English, and *Poeme din Zona de Tranzit, Antologie de Poezie Hispanică Contemporană* (*Poems from the Transit Zone An Anthology of Contemporary Hispanic Poetry*), (Tracus Arte, București, 2020) translated from Spanish. He translated into English poems by Mihai Eminescu, Nichita Stănescu and Nicolae Labiș and into Romanian poems by Octavio Paz, Cesar Vallejo, Roque Dalton, Abul Ala`a Al Ma`ari, Bhartrahari, René Char, Roger Gilbert-Lecomte, Sharon Mesmer, and others. He is the founder and editor-in-chief of Respiro, a cultural magazine active online 2000-2015 (www.respiro.org).

CLAUDIU KOMARTIN is a poet, translator, editor and anthologist. He has published seven collections of poetry. Since 2010, he is the editor-in-chief of the prestigious Poesis International magazine and of the Max Blecher Publishing House. He has edited over 150 books and several praised poetry anthologies and translated numerous authors from English, French and Spanish (Philippe Claudel, Le Clézio, Tahar Ben Jelloun, Kurt Vonnegut, Mario Benedetti etc.). He was vice-president of PEN Romania (2019-2023).